Spatialities
The Geographies of Art and Architecture

Edited by Judith Rugg and Craig Martin

D1354836

intellect Bristol, UK / Chicago, USA

First published in the UK in 2012 by
Intellect, The Mill, Parnall Road, Fishponds, Bristol, BS16 3JG, UK

First published in the USA in 2012 by
Intellect, The University of Chicago Press, 1427 E. 60th Street,
Chicago, IL 60637, USA

A catalogue record for this book is available from the
British Library.

Cover designer: Persephone Coelho
Copy-editor: Macmillan
Typesetting: John Teehan

ISBN 978-1-84150-468-1

Printed and bound by Hobbs, UK

Contents

Introduction

Judith Rugg

This book proposes 'spatialities' as a conceptual environment in which to consider the increasingly evolving concept of the spatial and its relevance to contemporary practice and theory in art, architecture and geography. It brings together artists, geographers, architects and cultural theorists who explore the inter-relationships between perceptual and material spatial fields through new frameworks of critical thinking. This book considers space not as a defining category, but as a migrating, uneven and entangled conceptual terrain of *spatiality* where conceptual structures are assembled and contested. These propose the tensions of space as both improvised and cohesive and within which interdisciplinary geographies and concepts of the spatial are made and unmade within various infrastructures of mobility. Contributors address the interstitial, the liminal and the relational as possible ways of locating positions for spatial reflection and representation as forms of encounter: transient, mobile and evolving.

The 14 chapters are assembled in four parts where a porosity of ideas takes place between a range of spatial disciplines. In Part I, 'Time, Landscape and Eroded Space,' artist Susan Collins and geographers Mike Crang and Tim Edensor explore the experience of place and time and its implications for the representation of landscape, architecture and the perception of events. Accumulations, assemblages, fleeting engagement, fluctuations and flows, issues of migration and displacement and the 'mobility of effect' become mechanisms for consideration and possibility to address the inherent instabilities of spatial representation.

In 'Unfolding Time: Pixel Landscapes, *Seascape* and the Aesthetics of Transmission,' Susan Collins explores the relationship between landscape and time, the balance of abstraction to representation and the moment of the 'now' in her work. In *Seascape*, web cameras were installed at various vantage points along the south coast of England, framing the horizon and transmitting and archiving seascape images in real time. Each image was constructed through a process of continuously evolving horizontal bands where individual pixels recorded fluctuations in light and tidal movement. Poised between the still and the moving image, using light and time, *Seascape* explored the possibilities of the experience of landscape space through coded and decoded images.

In 'Anne Tallentire's Timespaces in the Debris of Globalisation,' Mike Crang discusses the artist Anne Tallentire's installation, *Dimora*, in relation to issues of displacement, migrancy and globalisation. Situating the work with Castells' concept of 'spaces of flows' where place is conceived as a space in which to frame the movement of people, he considers the implications for the representation of spatiality for contemporary artists.

Crang proposes that *Dimora* offers views of fragments of makeshift intimate space, made habitable by minute processes of order that suggest events which are about to happen, rather than documenting those which have taken place. Accumulations and assemblages disclose imprints of absence and concealment: those caught within the flotsam of flows of migration. Tallentire's work can be perceived within this sense of fleetingness as a transient encounter offering a moment in time.

Tim Edensor's 'Materiality, Time and the City: the multiple temporalities of building stone' explores the relationship between time and the city by investigating the different temporalities suggested by one of its most common material ingredients. Understandings of place are confounded by the geological time embodied in stone and by looking at multiple temporalities we can avoid the tendency to produce reified, singular, linear accounts of urban time to reveal the innumerable processes through which cities are connected and ceaselessly recomposed.

Edensor develops an analysis of several ephemeral relationships conjured up by stone in the city of Manchester. He investigates how the city is endlessly reproduced by its connections with other places and how these networks are resonant within it. He explores the temporalities of the numerous agencies that assail stone and the buildings to which it belongs, eroding and decaying matter according to different contingencies at various rates. Edensor considers the way the past permeates into the present through the traces of human labour that reside in the substance of which buildings are made ; and where the rhythms of repair and maintenance act to freeze time by arresting decay and restoring the urban material fabric.

In Part II, 'Relational Reconfigurations', artists Jane Grant and John Matthias, geographer Tim Cresswell, art historian Dominic Rahtz and cultural theorist Craig Martin explore forms of topographies of space such as networks, voids and interstitial spaces, which are constructed by the possibilities of narrative, sound and the 'geographies of the in-between.' These are considered as part of wider intertwining processes of complexity, subject to and dependent on, varying forms of mobilities and perspectives. In 'Shifting Topographies: Sound and *The Fragmented Orchestra*', Jane Grant and John Matthias reflect on the huge sonic installation created with Nick Ryan and exhibited from December 2008 to February 2009 at FACT, Liverpool and at 23 other sites around the UK. They examine the topography of *The Fragmented Orchestra* and its embodiment of the cortical model, which is central to the work. A computer was host to a network of cortical neurons connected to 23 sites via the Internet and stimulated directly by sound, sending a dislocated fragment of the sound from its site to one of 24 speakers hanging from the ceiling in the gallery and to the other 23 sites and to the installation's website (www.thefragmentedorchestra.com).

In 'Ergin Çavuşoğlu and the Art of Betweeness', Tim Cresswell provides a geographical engagement with the art of Ergin Çavuşoğlu, who grew up in Bulgaria as part of a Turkish minority and now lives in London. His work, mostly in the form of video installations, has consistently sought to represent and reproduce the feeling of spaces 'in-between', evoking a mysterious entanglement of place and mobility that asks us to confront the ways in which they make and undo each other. Airport terminals, borders, ships at sea, towns cloaked in fog and anonymous spaces of the city feature in his work, as do things that travel, such as books or containers. Çavuşoğlu's art is an art of liminality that asks questions about how we make places in the space of flows and how these spaces are enmeshed.

In 'Daniel Buren's Theoretical Practice,' Dominic Rahtz explores Buren's work in the years around 1968, examining relationships among the artist's 1970 text 'Beware!', the impersonality of his work and the nature of its political character. Questions concerning relationships between art and action took on particular importance in 1968 during a period of, on the one hand, Rahtz argues, the impulse to act politically and on the other, by the need to separate art from action. The negation of form and impersonality in Buren's patterns of stripes and its siting across 100 street locations in Paris, questioned both its own appearance and its disappearance as 'object', producing new spaces of separateness and political possibility.

Within the rubric of contemporary mobility theory there exist varying assemblages of order and disorder, cohesion and non-cohesion and in 'Smuggler-Objects: The Material Culture of Alternative Mobilities' Craig Martin considers the appreciation of such competing forces, which tend towards a relational conception of time and space. Parasitic chains of connection operate within the geographies of contemporary capitalism whose flows of commodities, people and information are premised on the concerted attempt to filter out unwanted 'interferences' in its logic.

Acts of drug smuggling utilise these commodity chains as a means to parasite validated mobilities. This is seen in the figure of the human drug mule and in the form of smuggler objects where smuggling exploits qualities of commodity culture. Such objects are dependent on the relationship between visibility and invisibility in movements of commodity distribution and adapt 'innocent' artefacts such as toys. The tangled forces of drug smuggling operating within these legitimated mobilities are reliant on a form of parasitism where the infrastructure of sanctioned movement is infiltrated and utilised as a form of motive force.

Architectural photography can be a mechanism for the unfolding of urban place, which both asserts and contests belief in its own capacity to represent an imagined urban future. In Part III, 'Projected Utopias,' art theorist T. J. Demos, artists Layla Curtis and Steffi Klenz and photographer Nigel Green consider how photographic images of architecture can represent the city as a perpetual fantasised utopia. They discuss how order, idealisation and commodified space are values that are embedded within the architectural photograph and which make urban space readable and bound within limited terms. They propose an alternative, anti-aesthetic of photographic urban space as paradoxical, uncertain, fragmented and melancholic. Tracking, tracing and various ways of considering apprehensions of experiential spaces are explored as methodological approaches in their various investigations of the city.

In 'The Cruel Dialectic: on the work of Nils Norman' T. J Demos reflects on the artist Nils Norman's book *The Contemporary Picturesque* in relation to the global transformation of urban public space into a fortified zone of surveillance and 'body regulation.' Mostly black and white, Norman's images are anti-aesthetic, standing out against other artist-photographers who beautify public space through devices such as dramatic composition, the use of saturated colours and the production of high-quality prints. The term 'picturesque' invokes an ideal beauty but Nils Norman's book casts into relief the depressing reality that has turned urban space into a carceral zone in which to discipline and punish. It parodies contemporary art, which transforms scenes of domination into images of consumerism, and re-presents them as sublime typographies of masochistic desire, fostering critical viewpoints.

Layla Curtis's work constructs fictions and creates connections between things by appropriating place names, geography and cultural signifiers as abstract material. Her video works, collages and digitally generated drawings re-conceptualize the world as traceries of hidden histories of physicality and connection. Her video work, 'Traceurs: to trace, to draw, to go fast' used heat-seeking cameras to investigate alternative ways of mapping by tracking the routes of urban Parkours moving through the city, overcoming all obstacles in their path. Richard Grayson's essay explores relationships between architecture and the body in this new work, derived from *Traceurs* and located in a point between drawing, photography and film.

Through the series of photographs, *Nonsuch* and *Nummianus* Steffi Klenz explores concepts of boundaries and psychological space. These artworks document sites of architectural and social utopias such as Poundbury new town and frame a paradoxical relationship to place apparently not subject to time. In Klenz's work there is a sense of the process of an unfolding of urban place. The absence of people and the intense focus on detail create a confusion between artificial and real space, evoking questions of representation, value and belief in the practice of photographing the built environment.

With reference to his own photographic darkroom practice and the historic technique of hand-coloured photographs, in 'From the Melancholy Fragment to the Colour of Utopia: excess and representation in modernist architectural photography,' Nigel Green looks at the ways photographic-based imagery articulates ideas of the utopian through what he defines as 'modernist architectural space.' Through Husserl's concept of the *Lebenswelt* he argues that architectural photography can simultaneously be considered as being both inherently melancholic and utopian.

The idea of utopia as a desire to transform reality is similarly internal to that of the process of photography. Green's own photographic practice exploits the fugitive nature of traditional chemical-based black-and-white darkroom processes to produce images of modernist architecture that constitute a fragmentation of both subject and medium by situating the image within an uncertain readability. The hand-colouring of photographic postcards from pre-war World Fairs and Expositions, echo the processes at play in Green's 'fragment' images. Green explores how his own chemically produced 'fragments' and the historical practice of colouring black-and-white photographs by hand can be considered as supplementary in an 'excess of meaning.' These images are also transforming through what Walter Benjamin described as a process of 'deformation' revealing the utopian as always existing as a figure of the imaginary.

In Part IV 'Disrupted Concepts of "Home"', art theorist Judith Rugg, design historian Roni Brown and artist Lucy Harrison propose different ways of orientating space in its unpredictabilities. They consider the imbricated relationships between place, architecture and subjectivity where forms of cultural identity are bound by networks of memory, historical event and social activity. They probe how these relationships are architecturally situated, experienced and constructed and subject to decay and crisis, exploring the socio-political and formal contexts of identification between place, architecture and cultural meaning and finding it tenuous, fragile and subject to rupture.

In 'The Barbican: living in an airport without the fear of departure,' Judith Rugg considers the Barbican in the City of London and its oppositional relation between place and space created by its cathedral-like gloom, confusing signage and disorientating floor levels. Its bewildering expanse of architectural spaces could equally cause it to be likened to a cruise-ship, a prison, a department store or a hotel. Rugg reflects on the spatial paradox of living in the Barbican: its location within a global centre of corporate and financial power, surrounded by the endless building programme of the City and situated within a local authority that has its own police force and unique electoral system. If the City is an ongoing fantasy of desire for its corporate planners, the Barbican's architecture, with its highwalks and formal gardens, modelled on Le Corbusier's modernist utopia of the 'radiant city,' realizes the dream of the death of the street and the eradication of the unpredictability of human social relations.

In 'Defining Space – making space and telling stories: homes made by amateurs' Roni Brown considers the activity of 'self-build homes'. Research in material culture has been concerned with space as a representation of the social world, constituted by the relationship of people to systems of production and consumption. But there is a growing body of literature proposing that within the terms of commodification, spatial meaning is created by individuals through their personal agency and experience.

Brown contends that the amateur designing and making processes offer a useful arena for considering concepts of lived experience on the one hand, and the representation of the social world on the other. The home becomes both a series of formal problems to be solved and an autobiographical text, revealing how architecture can be an important social phenomenon in which people as well as buildings are 'made'. Brown shifts emphasis away from a consideration of 'home space' as an outcome of a design and building process, to one of 'home-making' as a thoroughly situated social activity.

The artist Lucy Harrison's work is concerned with the subjective nature of our relationship to places and how understanding of place is often bound to individual memory and experience. In 'Remains,' she reflects on how she is drawn to scenes of devastation such as demolition sites, and their potential for metaphorical meaning about unfulfilled dreams or political ideals. Presenting a series of images of despoiled places of leisure – abandoned cinemas, theatres and nightclubs – Harrison considers how these contemporary images have become associated with historical ones such as archival photographs of the Blitz in 1944. She proposes that like architecture, social relations are also fragile and subject to assaults such as that of forgetting, rupture and conflict, all of which have the capacity to destroy networks and the meanings of place.

The chapters' different intonations on the consideration of the spatial reflect the authors' backgrounds as artists, architects, geographers and theorists and propose a diversity of resonances and focus. The book's range of disciplinary perspectives offers different approaches through which to consider the critical aspects of space and its span incorporates contemplative and academic strategies as well as conversations and reflections on practice. It presents a confluence of experience, configurations and modes of writing registers as forms of correlation for the consideration of space as *spatiality* – a territory of thinking, writing and making.

Part I

Time, Landscape and Eroded Space

Chapter 1

Unfolding Time: Landscapes, Seascapes and the Aesthetics of Transmission

Susan Collins

Figure 1: *Seascape* (2008–09).

From spring 2008 to summer 2009, network cameras were installed at five locations along the south-east coast of England from Margate to Gosport. Each camera looked out over the English Channel, framing the horizon and forming part of the panoramic series, *Seascape*. Transmitting and archiving in real time, each *Seascape* image was constructed pixel by pixel in horizontal bands continuously from top to bottom and left to right. Each complete image was collected over just under seven hours, recording the fluctuations in light and movement, time and tide throughout day and night.

Seascape (2008–09) built upon previous works *Fenlandia* (2004–05) and *Glenlandia* (2005–07) which explored the relationship between landscape and technological innovation in the areas known as Silicon Fen in Cambridgeshire and Silicon Glen in Scotland through a series of gradually unfolding, classically romantic landscape images that were harvested and archived over a number of years. *Seascape* extended the investigation to a less obviously picturesque and more abstracted depiction of time and tide.

This chapter will reflect on all three works: *Fenlandia*, *Glenlandia* and *Seascape*. It will explore issues raised by the works including the relationship between landscape and time; abstraction and representation; the aesthetics of transmission, and the moment of 'right now' in the work.

Time and transmission

This series of works found its origins in 2002 when I was developing the work, *Transporting Skies* (http://www.susan-collins.net/2002/transporting-skies), which relayed a live video image of sky between the two locations of Site Gallery in Sheffield, Yorkshire and Newlyn Art Gallery in Cornwall. The transmitted skies were projected on a large scale according to the architecture of each gallery, with each sky projection effectively providing a remote light source for the alternate location. The exhibition took place in November when the days in northern Sheffield were noticeably shorter than in Newlyn on the south-west coast, so that the projection of the Cornish sky at Site Gallery would show daylight for some time after it had grown dark outside. At twilight, the transmission process became more apparent, with the pixelated compressed digitization of the streamed sky taking on a certain abstract, painterly, Klimt-like visual quality. Parts of the images buffered and lingered, creating an almost liquid effect on the staggered, streamed image. The darkness took on distinct qualities for each location: in urban Sheffield, the light pollution gave a permanently reddish hue, whereas the night sky in rural Newlyn became unambiguously pitch black.

A second work also provided a live connection between the two galleries. Intended to locate the work more specifically to Sheffield and Newlyn, I was influenced by the fact that the first transatlantic Morse code message was transmitted by Marconi from Cornwall, and more pragmatically by the very little bandwidth I had left to play with after the live video exchange of sky. I wondered how I might transmit images or information live in real time between the two places in a way that used only the very smallest amount of data, initially exploring the possibility of transmitting an image by Morse code. I speculated on how long it would take and what it might look like, and it is this that led

Figure 2: *Penzance*, 15th November 2002.

to the development of my first pixel-landscape work, employing the pixel as the unit of transmission, instead of a dot or dash.

Using basic desktop webcams, images were transmitted between the two locations via the internet. A program updated the images a pixel every second, starting in the top left-hand corner of the screen and writing horizontally, like text on a page until reaching the bottom right-hand corner, when it would start again, writing over the previous image, continuously. The images were a low resolution of 320 × 240, so that at the rate of a pixel a second, a whole image was made up of individual pixels collected over 76,800 seconds (or 21.33 hours), taking just less than a day to complete.

A pure experiment, it was hard to predict when installing the work how these images might actually look or what they might reveal. In constructing the image in this way over time, the permanent and the ephemeral become more apparent. The presence of a passing bird, person, car or other object for instance, appeared as stray pixels, miniscule interruptions in the image; whereas in Newlyn night time appeared as a strong band of black with only the lights of Penzance puncturing the darkness [fig. 2]. In both locations, the normally subtle fluctuations in light throughout the course of the day became immediately apparent in the banding effect that appears in the images.

In both these works, time and the network together contributed to both the fabric and unfolding of the work.

Time and place

The following year, I was commissioned by Film and Video Umbrella to make a piece of work in response to the area in East Anglia known as Silicon Fen. This is an area where in addition to the cluster of new and emerging technology companies (from which it gets its name), technology is literally embedded in the flat horizons, which evidence an earlier technological age, a reclaimed landscape of canals, sluices, dykes and ditches. This presented an opportunity to marry the horizontality of the pixel landscapes to their subject – the fens being very flat – and to develop the work further by creating an online version, whilst also archiving and harvesting images over the course of a full year.

A networked camera was installed on the roof of The Anchor Inn, a seventeenth century coaching inn in Sutton Gault, Cambridgeshire overlooking the New Bedford River in the heart of Silicon Fen. The resulting work, *Fenlandia*, was live online for 12 months from May 2004 to May 2005 [fig. 3].

The camera sent a continuous stream of images to a server in London through the Internet. Using the same technique as the previous experiment, a program then constructed images at the rate of a pixel a second from top to bottom of the screen in horizontal bands, continuously. As before, the images were low resolution, each taking 21.33 hours or just less than a day to 'complete'.

Figure 3: *Fenlandia*, 30th June 2004 at 20:43 pm.

A further, Scottish 'sister' version, *Glenlandia*, named after Scotland's notional 'Silicon Glen' was live from the end of August 2005 for two years. Whereas *Fenlandia* recorded minute changes in the Fen landscape of eastern England, *Glenlandia* instead looked out over Loch Faskally, in Perthshire, Scotland – a place where technology is also implicitly embedded in the landscape.

Appearing to exemplify a quintessentially natural Scottish landscape, Loch Faskally is in fact man-made, constructed to service a hydroelectric dam in Pitlochry which in turn supplies all the power for the surrounding area. The water levels in the Loch rise and fall regularly (and sometimes dramatically) according to the level of demand for electricity in the neighbouring glens [fig. 4].

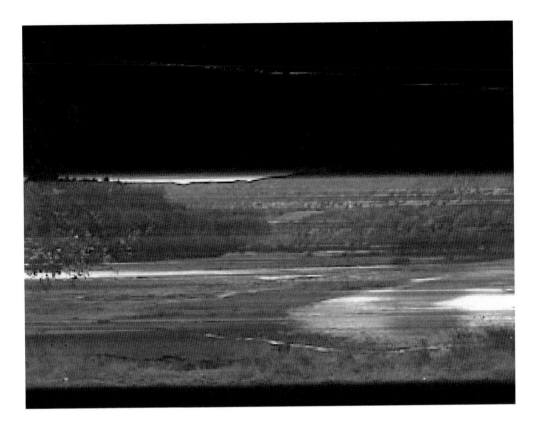

Figure 4: *Glenlandia*, 16th September 2005 at 11:04 am
revealing an empty Loch Faskally.

Both *Fenlandia* and *Glenlandia* existed in different forms: a 'live' version and a still version. The 'live' version consisted of a full-screen landscape image transmitting live in real time that was displayed as a gallery installation [fig. 5]. Viewers could also download display software from the project websites (http://www.susan-collins.net/fenlandia and http://www.susan-collins.net/glenlandia) so that they could view the landscape updating online in real time, pixel by pixel, full screen on any computer.

Images from both *Fenlandia* and *Glenlandia* were saved at 2 hour intervals creating a complete archive of just under 4000 and 8000 images, respectively. The 'still' manifestation of the works is derived from these archives and presented in the form of small and large-format digital prints. Both versions, the *live* and the *still*, have something distinct to offer.

Figure 5: *Glenlandia* installed at Oakville Galleries, Ontario looking out over gardens and Lake Ontario beyond, transmitting a piece of Scotland live into the Canadian landscape.

Colour, revealed by each individual pixel, is foregrounded in the prints. In general, the larger format prints serve to deconstruct the image, exposing the variations between each individual pixel: the black of night time that is made up of many blacks; pink or blue sunrises, and many kinds of yellow, orange, ochre and green in between. The smaller prints when lined up together in series expose a sense of duration, revealing a range of shifts and changes: from the thinning and widening band of black (night time) showing the lengthening and shortening days throughout the year, to the full moon that *Glenlandia* has occasionally captured and which appears as if a white comet streaking through the night sky but is in fact the moon slipping through the image over time [fig. 6].

I consider this work as a kind of 'open system:' one inhabited and activated by light, day, night, weather, movement of the sun, the moon, the seasons and all these analogue variables that conspire to produce an infinite variety of unique images.

Figure 6: *Glenlandia*, 19th August 2005 at 09:53 am.

Yet, there are also human interventions (beyond stray pixel appearances), which make themselves visible. On 20th December 2004 in *Fenlandia*, the tree to the left of the image mysteriously disappeared from view. Initially, I thought the camera may have moved in strong winds; however, all the other landmarks were still *in situ*. I found out later that the tree had been chopped down because of subsidence and all the *Fenlandia* images produced thereafter have a bleaker, more abstract and less Arcadian feel to them [fig. 7].

Fenlandia and *Glenlandia* deliberately trade on the convention – or rather the perceived convention – of how a landscape image might historically have been composed and constructed. The landscape image is recorded absolutely as the camera sees it, and the results are read as a landscape, but because of the time shift the image is simultaneously both recognizable and unrecognizable.

Figure 7: *Fenlandia*, 28th March 2005 at 08:41 am.

Time and again

I was interested in developing further this potential for abstraction in the work, and I began looking at the seascape as a potential subject while artist in residence at Monash University in Melbourne in 2006; experimenting by constructing images from Australian 'surfcams' – the webcams set up on surfer beaches to let the surfers know when the surfing is good. Subsequently, I was invited to develop this still further with Film and Video Umbrella and the De La Warr Pavilion, Bexhill-on-Sea, a modernist icon on the south-east coast of England whose long wall of picture windows looks directly out to sea. The result was *Seascape* (http://www.susan-collins.net/seascape): a panorama of live feeds constructing images slowly over time from five locations across the south-east coast of England over the course of a year.

Between March and October 2008, networked cameras were installed at different vantage points along the coast: at Margate, Folkestone, Bexhill-on-Sea, Pagham (near Bognor Regis) and Stokes Bay (near Gosport). In seeking the potential for abstraction, I set the view for each camera to frame the sea and sky with a common horizon line and largely evacuated landmark features from the images. Sea and sky often became interchangeable, creating false horizons through the horizontal construction of the image combined with fast changing light and weather conditions.

Figure 8: *Seascape*, Stokes Bay, 27th September 2008 at 14:13 pm.

The individual characteristics of each location emerged over time. In Bexhill-on-Sea and Folkestone, the relationship between sea and shoreline remained virtually constant, whereas in Margate and Pagham underlying topographical features (seaweed and a sunken WW2 Mulberry, respectively) were repeatedly disclosed by the ebb and flow of the tide. Passing traffic was evident to a greater or lesser extent in each location. In Margate, lights from anchored ships were captured on the horizon at night time, whereas at Stokes Bay the evidence of numerous stray pixels testified to a busy waterway of passing ships, yachts, people and windsurfers [fig. 8].

Each image became a slice or section of the continuous panorama that is the south-east coast with each whole image made from individual pixels collected over just less than seven hours, approximately the time it takes for the tide to come in or go out.

For the exhibition at the De La Warr Pavilion, five live projections showing the seascapes being constructed in real time were projected into the windows, against the backdrop of the actual, live coast itself [fig. 9].

Figure 9: Installation view, *Seascape*, De La Warr Pavilion, Bexhill-on-Sea, 2009. Photo credit: Joe Clark.

A series of still images from the *Seascape* archive were exhibited as digital prints alongside the live projections to give a sense of not only the variations between the different locations, but the variations in the same location from month-to-month, day-to-day and even moment-to-moment.

The process of observation is distinct for the live and the still images. When looking at the live image there is an active engagement. The 'now' moment is constantly moving, it is in flux; a still image that is constantly changing. It could be seen effectively as a moving still, focusing on the 'now' moment, often mesmerizing with its slowness and this concentration on finding and then following one tiny moving pixel. In the moving still, the point of 'right now' shifts constantly through each image, whereas the prints, stills the

Figure 10: *Seascape*, Folkestone, 25th October 2008 at 11:41 am.

'right now' as the moment and the point at which that image is captured or archived. The prints become by contrast more contemplative; less concerned with seeking the moving pixel, they are ripe for decoding and recognizing the colour of each individual pixel as a distinct moment in time and space.

Whilst this process reveals some things such as the movement of the moon through the sky in *Glenlandia*, it misses others. For instance, in *Seascape*, the most violent lightning storm would appear as just a few stray pixels giving away little sense of a turbulent sea. A *re*-presentation of a familiar subject, it is reality but not as one normally witnesses it. Six or seven hours compresses into a single frame, time shifts, and while the source for the image may have come from a landscape or seascape, the image has the potential to become autonomous, something else, with the accrual of the image over time bringing its own set of artefacts and abstractions.

Time-lapsed images provide a unique opportunity to reveal those things that we may be aware of and yet happen too slowly for us to consciously observe. For all of these works, time becomes embedded as each image is slowly revealed within a continuously updating time-lapse film caught within a single frame. Poised between the still and the moving image, the lens and the pixel, these images become coded and decoded using light and time, rendering the familiar unfamiliar and potentially providing an opportunity to question, reframe and reinterpret our often routine relationship with the physical world.

Chapter 2

Timespaces in the Debris of Globalization

Mike Crang

Figure 1: Anne Tallentire, *Dimora* (2006), c-print, 59.3 cm × 42 cm, collection Biblioteca Panizzi, Reggio Emilia.

A good place to start this chapter is by thinking about particularly the *Dimora* works and how they fit in the overall arc of work that addresses displacement, globalization and so forth. What I think the *Dimora* series offers is pictures that are speaking to a space of globalization, a space of globality; and that they are speaking about migrant workers, the international labour economy and alongside that, they imply the ever more problematic international flows of capital and so on, that both drive, enable and are supported by those flows of people. They illustrate what Manuel Castells (1996) has called a world comprised of 'spaces of flows' rather than places. And I think it is interesting then to think how do we represent, depict or imagine that sort of spatiality because I think what Anne Tallentire's work gives is a very particular form of spatialization to try and think through that world in flow.

Through her 'photositings' of various sorts, Tallentire is producing particular types of spaces that speak to and illuminate those issues in very particular ways. They take their cue from Georges Perec's (1997) work, to offer a *Species of Spaces*. They transport us to, or perhaps better, only afford a glimpse into, a series of specific spaces seen as discrete, relatively self-contained microcosms or, in geography's technical vocabulary, particular sorts of time-space locales. This builds on the sense of estrangement in the moving versions of her *Drift* (2002–2010) series that for instance, decelerate activity and stress repetition to show activities that characterize these time-spaces – what we might call the modes of inhabitation of these spaces. The media allow us to exceed natural vision, either by enlargement or extending events in time, and as Benjamin long ago pointed out, this transforms our apperception of our space and time: 'Our taverns and our metropolitan streets, our offices and furnished rooms, our railroad stations and our factories appeared to have us locked up hopelessly. Then came the film and burst this prison-world asunder by the dynamite of the tenth of a second, so that now, in the midst of its far-flung ruins and debris, we calmly and adventurously go travelling. With the close-up, space expands; with slow motion, movement is extended. The enlargement of a snapshot does not simply render more precise what in any case was visible, though unclear: it reveals entirely new structural formations of the subject. So, too, slow motion not only presents familiar qualities of rapid movements, but give the effect of singularly gliding, floating, supernatural motions' (Walter Benjamin 1973: 239). I quote this at length because the work here perhaps finds a world already broken up amidst the familiar and explores the debris and ruins of times and spaces left by modern life. It does not simply reveal the actions and practices of people more precisely – but estranges and transforms them to reveal the fabrication of our habituated world. I think what this strategy of estrangement and discrete spaces enables Anne Tallentire to try and create in the *Dimora* series is a non-totalizing version of a global space.

I say this because there are some iconic and very easy ways of depicting globality as a totality – grasping the global flows highlighted by Castells. There are well-known pictures of electrons zooming around, or data flows looping over the globe. These visualizations are indeed actually quite hard to produce but they make global process apprehensible as a totality. What is offered in Tallentire's *Dimora* series instead is not a sort of holistic depiction of the system but rather the fragments of an intimate personal sort of space. These are spaces that are characterized by what is done, how they are used, how people in whatever makeshift ways inhabit them. These are, in Michel de Certeau's (1984) terms, 'practiced spaces'. The pictures are about spaces where things are being made to happen, where things are going on. It is quite important that these are not just the ordered places of particular regimes of knowledge or capital or labour or whatever it may be: they are not the planned and controlled representations of global processes, but exceed or undercut those representational controls.

Tallentire's work achieves that through its focus on the micro-arrangements, accommodations and adaptations she finds. So in *Drift*, the focus on bodily comportment and the notion of bodily hexis or gait, opens a way of thinking through how people inhabit the space at a level of embodied dwelling. In the *Dimora* sequence, we might see the same effect through the assemblages of things that yet bear the trace of their absent makers. Thus, at first sight what appear to be a number of pictures of a happenstance accumulation of objects (car bonnet, chipboard, bucket and car parcel shelf) (Figure 1) turn out to be pictures of the same assemblage from different angles (Figures 2 & 3). In fact, is it a sleeping shelter for an illegal migrant artfully camouflaged amid the post-industrial debris to look like any accidental bundle of materials? It shows the imprint of life, in that from these materials are formed little shelters that are also decoys, concealment and are thus quite carefully arranged. In choosing this, it seems to me that the pictures speak to an absent presence of the migrants, of the flows of capital and systems of control. They speak to the limits of control over the migrants and their struggles to control their own destiny. They highlight the intricate coming together of what appears to be just the happenstance flotsam of international migration. But I think what is interesting is, that Tallentire's work avoids what I would end up doing which is depicting the obvious, depicting presence, the alien bodies of the migrant in our European space. I come from a discipline that would want an illustration of what is going on – if you want to show migrant work then it would want lots of pictures of workers doing work, preferably the most obviously global workers doing work. And that is exactly what is not shown here. These are not pictures showing oppression or exploitation. They draw back from the obvious, so they do not actually represent what they are speaking about.

Coupled with this refusal to show, is the low-fi aesthetic, almost anti-aesthetic, of the pictures. In Tallentire's *Villagio* (2008) sequence of railway worker camps, there is a sort of low-fi snap-shot aesthetic. That seems to, first, de-privilege the mode of representation or at least the notion of the auteur, as offering a new way of seeing. It draws upon the currency of the snapshot which for all of us is a way of trying to convey the feel of a place and a sense of documenting immediate contact. Yet, second, the approach creates a sense of fleetingness in these spaces. Here, the transient encounter producing the picture parallels the transient people and nature of the spaces. They offer but a moment in time and a small pocket in space neither of which will endure.

In choosing the ironic name 'Village,' the sequence also foregrounds a contrast of these makeshift and momentary spaces with the classic organic community depicted by the classic anthropologists that depend on some sense of being an enduring, self-contained, detached whole, which quite clearly this is anything but. In this sense, I am enormously pleased that this work does not fall into the sort of traps set up by someone like Marc Augé (1995) in his theorization of non-spaces where he counterposes spaces of hyper modernity – modernity not being good enough anymore – to precisely that

Figure 2. *Dimora*. c-print, 59.3 cm × 42 cm,
collection Biblioteca Panizzi, Reggio Emilia.

sense of organic community. Non-spaces, which he exemplifies with supermarkets, petrol stations and airports, are all governed by anonymous contact where we strip down the signifying layers. They are thin on resonance but large on injunction. We can all think of places that are sort of like that except I think what these pictures show is that, even when we strip down those signifying layers, what we find are not empty non-places, but places made habitable by people; they are indeed inhabited in the strongest sense. The pictures here follow the anthropological injunction of Clifford Geertz (1993) to move from megaconcepts to micrological examination, to recall that although we may study *in* villages, we do not study villages – that is, among homely locations and forms, we may find the grand concepts and processes.

Yet, these pictures also resist romanticizing dwelling in these transient spaces – they are unhomely. *Villagio* perhaps invokes a species of space that speaks most strongly to Georgio Agamben's (1998) space of the camp; the space of exception, beyond the law for those not included in society or afforded its protective embrace. *Villagio* is the migrant workers' camp, designed to be set up, taken down, moved on and set up again elsewhere. Here, if anywhere one overwhelming order would seem to impose itself within those boundaries, leaving nothing but the bare life of exploited labour. And yet, these pictures suggest the camp does not leave just bare life. Much work following Agamben has highlighted the bio-politics of bare life in policing migrants and asylum seekers; it points to the history of the camp as a space of exception; outwith the usual social rules, a space that both contains and produces the *homo sacer* of classic Roman doctrine – the life without rights. In South Africa, workers express their fear of people turned into zombies after bosses 'sucked away their human essence and turned them into brute labour power; this to make them toil away at night in the fields' (Comaroff & Comarroff 2003, page 149). But what is important here is that these pictures do not then follow the obvious route of focusing on the people concentrating on bare life through their bodies – be they abject, rendered docile or labouring. Instead, they work through the spaces and truly these spaces shape the limits of migrant workers' rights.

Villagio shows the licensed and constrained spaces of the camp where legal workers are allowed. One might compare and contrast those spaces with the makeshift camps, such as the Roma camp on the via Malibran; or under the flyovers outside the working class suburb of Ponticelli, east of Naples, which was burnt down by the locals; or the six run-down apartment buildings in Padua inhabited by North African immigrants that have come to be known as Via Anelli Ghetto after they were walled by order of the mayor; or the hidden spaces of the illegal migrant workers in *Dimora*. Each expresses a different modality of space and inhabitation. The limited, circumscribed and flickering possibilities to make these spaces liveable comes through in these picures partially in the absence of life but also in the fleeting traces of it contained in the pictures.

There is one person tucked away in one of these pictures – just the back of them manages to sneak in. The people are otherwise not there; so they start to speak to the conditions about bare life rather than making a too obvious emotive appeal on a sort of humanistic level. There are just the hints of life made bearable. In one of the *Dimora* pictures, in the corner you can just about make out the football which is quite clearly what people have been kicking about and, if you persevere, you can make out what were used for the goalposts. So here you have concealment and hidden dwelling but also the beautiful game. I am not saying that this makes it a happy, lovely place but it speaks to the possibilities of just recovering something of these people as people through their own agency and doings. But not representing the people directly is an important open political move because what that does is embody the social invisibility of those people. It stages the absence, hiding and thus shows that these are the hidden workers, the hidden migrants and the invisible flows of globalization. These people will not get a 700 million dollar bail-out because global flows cause a crisis; these are the underside, the dark side of globalization and so, by not showing them I think the pictures stage their very condition of invisibility rather than the more obvious move of trying to make them visible.

That latter notion of using photography to bring to light what was hidden, in a very different way than is done here, is problematic because that is exactly what the state attempts to do on so many occasions. The state invests in representational technologies to make illegal migrants visible, trackable, taggable and thus deportable.

Ursula Biemann's video work, *Remote Sensing* (2001, 2002) about trafficked women highlights this duality of self-representation and surveillant visuality with her split screens combining the exact locational technologies of GPS mapping along with the images of freedom dreamt by the women and the images of sexualization through which they are sold. Tallentire's *Viallagio* spaces would similarly seem apt for such multiple competing locational frames. They are heterotopias – a multi-coded space of competing ordering systems. The imposed order of the company directors stands against a counter order with a different set of orderings from the workers and you have another imaginary imposed order from locals who seek to pen-off or limit the camp. The work here chooses a different path from Biemann. Instead of multiplying the representational registers it attenuates them. It renders the migrants inaccessible yet present and in so doing, opens a productive political space to 'speak' to that spatiality of globalization, as clashing orders in heterotopic sites, more akin to Allan Sekula's (1995) wonderful book, *Fish Story* that traces global flows through the shipping trade, allowing him to depict both the epic scale and substance of global trade, with an additional political charge through the tragic–comic juxtaposition of great and small, near and far and of different orders colliding in place.

Tallentire's works resonate and contrast with other pictures of deserted buildings. There are echoes of the sort of absences in Alison Marchant's *Charged Atmospheres* (1998), where there is a sense of places of absence, inhabited by a haunting and ghostly presence. Marchant's photographs, made from found negatives of the cataloguing of dilapidated and imperilled listed buildings of England, have a clearly melancholy charge, as they depict abandoned, formerly ornate, even glamorous, interiors. A sense of fragility, indeed of a time out of joint, is redoubled because not only are the interiors trashed,

Figure 3. *Dimora*, c-print, 59.3 cm × 42 cm,
collection Biblioteca Panizzi, Reggio Emilia.

and there is a question over whether they will be preserved, but even the pictures have been discarded: the documents of bureaucracy of the national monuments office have been chucked in a skip and are themselves scarred. The vision of absence, where one can make out the outline of a chest through the discoloured wall and of lost life seem to echo the sort of nostalgic view of old Paris in something like Atget's photography of old and vanishing Paris. It is the sense that what Walter Benjamin describes as pictures like the scene of a crime – always deserted and after the fact. Such specific temporal charge is an interesting contrast with the more flat aesthetic in Tallentire's work which resists the powerful emotive pull of the picturesque; resisting investing these spaces with a romantic charge. Both Marchant's and Tallentire's works also contrast with Tim Edensor's (2005) terms of looking at disused industrial sites as a form of modern ruin that can be read through a discourse of picturesque decay and loss to tell stories of the former lives of labour. This last offers a world haunted by the ghost of the British working class but not the ghost workers in the current global system.

Anne Tallentire's images seem to be presenting moments where globalization has been: they are the traces and containers that result from, enable and frame the translocated lives of migrants. They speak to the intrusion of the global into small spaces, yet also refuse to represent it. Their micrological view of global processes offers us a way to approach the incoherence of contemporary urban spaces, beneath the fantasies of community and globality. They show an absent presence, where the traces of workers speak to making bare life, barely liveable.

References

Agamben, Giogio and Heller-Roazan, D. (1998), *Homo Sacer: Sovereign Power and Bare Life*, Stanford: Stanford University Press.

Augé, Marc (1995), *Non-Places: Introduction to an Anthropology of Supermodernity*, London: Verso.

Benjamin, Walter (1973), 'The Work of Art in the Age of Mechanical Reproduction', Illuminations, London: Verso, pp. 211–244.

Biemann, Ursula (2001), 'Remotely Sensed: A Topography of the Global Sex Trade', *Feminist Review*, 70, pp. 75–88.

Biemann, Ursula (2002), 'Touring, Routing and Trafficking Female Geobodies: A Video Essay on the Topography of the Global Sex Trade', *Thamyris*, 9, pp. 71–86.

Castells, Manuel (1996), *The Rise of the Network Society: Networks and Identity*, Blackwell: Oxford.

de Certeau, Michel (1984), *The Practice of Everyday Life*, Berkeley: University of California Press.

Comaroff, J. and J. Comaroff (2003), "Ethnography on an Awkward Scale: Postcolonial Anthropology and the Violence of Abstraction." *Ethnography* 4(2): 147-80.

Edensor, Tim (2005), *Industrial Ruins: spaces, aesthetics, and materiality*, Oxford: Verso.

Geertz, Clifford (1993), *The Interpretation of Cultures: Selected Essays*, London: Basic Books.

Nesbit, Molly (1993), *Atget's Seven Albums*, New Haven: Yale University Press.

Perec, Georges (1997), *Species of Space and Other Pieces*, translated and edited by John Sturrock, London: Penguin.

Sekula, Allan (1995), *Fish Story*, Dusseldorf: Grin Verlag.

Chapter 3

Materiality, Time and the City: The Multiple Temporalities of Building Stone

Tim Edensor

Figure 1. St Anne's Church, Manchester.

Introduction

A building is a condensation of skilled activity that undergoes continual formation even as it is inhabited, that it incorporates materials that have life histories of their own and may have served time in previous structures, living and non-living, that it is simultaneously enclosed and open to the world, that it may be only semi-permanently fixed in place...

(Ingold 2004: 240)

This chapter explores the relationship between time and the city by investigating the different temporalities suggested by one of its most common material ingredients, building stone. By looking at these multiple and coinciding temporalities, we can avoid the tendency to produce reified, singular, linear accounts of urban time and reveal the innumerable temporal processes through which cities are connected and ceaselessly recomposed. The chapter investigates the stony temporalities of one central Manchester building, St Ann's Church, built in 1709. St Ann's remains an active ecclesiastical structure, and besides continuously changing, has been part of a bigger local collage in which its situatedness contrasts with the relative transience of surrounding buildings, surfaces and spatial functions (see Edensor and Drew 2007, for further images of the church). It has outlasted all surrounding buildings and is an enduring symbol of a post-industrial city which the violence of capitalist transformation has successively reconfigured.

After a brief discussion of time and urban materiality, I discuss how notions of place are complicated by the geological time embodied in stone. Secondly, I consider how the city is endlessly reproduced by its connections with other places, in this case with sites that have supplied stone for its (re)production, and I explore how these connections have been constituted at different spatial and temporal scales. Thirdly, I examine the temporalities of the numerous agencies which assail stone and the building to which it belongs, eroding and decaying matter according to different contingencies and at various rates. Fourthly, I look at how the rhythms of repair and maintenance act to freeze time by arresting decay and restoring urban material fabric, but also mark time of buildings. I conclude by looking at the way the past bursts into the present by invoking the metaphor of haunting to draw attention to the traces of humans and non-humans etched onto building stone, and by raising questions about how to conserve buildings that evoke such multiple temporalities.

Time and urban materiality

Although Dodgson (2008: 1) asserts that in the social sciences 'we can no longer draw on an overarching concept of time,' understandings and practices that temporally fix buildings and the places to which they belong. Orthodox and official narratives composed and reiterated by archaeologists, historians and place-sellers are usually shaped by a linear chronological progression through which key moments in a building's history are identified and the unfolding of the structure as it is today through successive decades and centuries are represented as a complete vestige of earlier times, 'encoded as if preserved at a particular juncture' (DeSilvey 2011). St Ann's Church is represented as a timeless fixture in the teleological narrative on the church's official website (stannsmanchester.com), where a succession of discrete eras and events form a solidified temporal framework. Where a building is of symbolic importance, as with St Ann's, one of three stone buildings in central Manchester to have outlasted the dynamic processes urban change to which the city has been subjected since the seventeenth century (the other two are the cathedral and Chetham's School), it is enrolled to foreground the 'timeless' qualities of continuity and stability, and forecloses speculation about the past by implying that it now appears 'as it was and ever shall be' (DeSilvey 2011). The picturesque qualities of the church similarly fix the building as an object for visual consumption, by tourists and shoppers, and furthermore, are utilized to tether memory to place, testifying to its singularity and suggesting a timelessness and an unbroken line from then to now. This evokes how specific 'memoryscapes', 'rhetorical topoi' and iconographic forms and commemorative stages are managed by power to organize a relationship with the past (Boyer 1996).

In challenging these representational fixings of time and place, this account foregrounds the dynamic, multiple and heterogeneous temporalities of the building. I follow May and Thrift's (2001: 5) contention that rather than being seduced by narratives that purvey a linear, 'singular or uniform social time stretching across a uniform social space', we need to be 'aware of various (and uneven) networks of time stretching in different and divergent directions across an uneven social field' and Barbara Adam's (1998: 202) advice to acknowledge the multiple, various and distinct formations of 'tempo, timing, duration, sequence and rhythm that are the mutually implicating structures of time.'

These distinct formations are materialized in the city, and more specifically, in the buildings that bear traces of the different people, processes and products that have circulated through their environs at different times. Diverse rates of material transformation and social change mean that some spaces and objects are erased whereas others remain. Kevin Lynch (1972: 171) famously contends that the city is subjected to continuous recomposition through the 'accumulation of overlapping traces from successive periods, each trace modifying and being modified by the new additions, to produce something like a collage of time.' Crang and Travlou (2001: 137) show how these juxtapositions in the materialities of Athens produce a pluritemporal landscape, 'not in the sense of a continuous historical narrative but as discordant moments sustained through a mosaic of sites where qualitatively different times interrupt spatialized juxtastructures.' The church that I explore is also an emergent mosaic of various temporalities. These urban materialities thus refute linear narratives that feature an unfolding succession of stories by the host of intersecting temporalities which 'collide and merge' in a landscape of juxtaposed 'asynchronous moments,' a spatialization of memory that involves 'crossing, folding, piercing' (Crang and Travlou 2001: 161) rather than sequential organization. These temporal collages reveal the emergent character of the elements within an assemblage of incessant becoming.

Over their lives, buildings are used for different purposes, aesthetically appraised according to contemporary tastes, demolished, renovated, amended, and spatially recontextualized by the erection of adjacent structures and planning redesignations. They are extended and reduced, are cannibalized, their textures change as they decay and disintegrate, and their meanings transform as earlier tastes and knowledge about their construction, purpose, design and symbolic qualities are superseded. Accordingly, buildings must be 'continually modified and adapted to fit in with manifold and ever-shifting purposes' (Ingold and Hallam 2007: 4) or drawn into new heterogeneous associations and networks (Bouzarovski 2009).

Despite these temporal vagaries, iconic buildings often serve to stabilize notions of place. Yet, such ordering processes involve 'the coordination of a large heterogeneity of material and immaterial elements into specific spatiotemporal arrangements' (Schwanen 2007: 12) to provide an illusion of security and permanence in the urban landscape, to reproduce pockets of local order in space. Such efforts are always provisional because they are always liable to be further modified by human action, and also because there are unrecognized potentialities in matter and often unforeseen and invisible agencies that assail it. Accordingly, although the constituent elements of a heterogeneous building assemblage are enrolled to stabilize space and materiality, they are invariably susceptible to entropy and disordering, and a continuously emergence, surrounded by so many relationalities and potentialities that it can never constitute any seamless whole over time.

The destiny of stone over time, like all matter, is partly shaped by its 'incipient tendencies or a certain capacity to self arrange, tendencies that are variously enacted depending upon the other forces, affects or bodies with which it comes into intimate physical contact' (Bennett 2008). Nevertheless, despite this continual change, stone is often 'the most durable element of the archaeological record' (Hurcombe 2007: 146), less evanescent than many other elements that are moved from elsewhere to stabilize a place. Winkler (1994: 2) identifies a diverse range of properties that make particular kinds of stone suitable as a construction material: the size and shape of the grains, their collective density and evenness, colour and colour stability, a resistance to indentation and abrasion, compressive strength, a capacity to absorb heat and cold, andresistance to acid rain, especially in urban environments. However, whatever these properties, the human and non-human agencies that will impact upon stone when it becomes part of a building assemblage can shorten or lengthen its life as constituent.

Geological time

The first temporal scale I explore is that of geological time for the length for which a building stone occupies a role as a building constituent, is of course, extremely brief when its age of origin is taken into account. As Yussof and Gabrys (2006: 447) remind us about our conceptions of place, 'what we take for solid rock and hard ground, the supposed permanence of site, is no more than papier mache in the scale of geological time.' Material change occurs at an enormously diverse range of temporal scales across human and non-human worlds and this extended sense of geological time situates our own temporal perspective of stability and change in the environment of which we are part because the processes of material change of stone are slow compared with the ageing of human bodies.

Despite the tendency to imagine a pre-historic past divided into different phases, eras and periods of stability, Massey (2006) insists that there can have been no settled pre-human past for moments of rupture, endurance, turbulence and fluidity occur randomly. Such temporalities are embodied in the materialities of stone and the trained geological eye can identify other times and places, summon up dramatic episodes and vistas in which floods surge across parched land, earthquakes disaggregate landscapes and volcanic eruptions shower down magma. In seas and rivers, a whole bestiary of life forms live, die, flow and settle as part of emergent sediments, ferocious rainfall and wind lash pre-existing rocks, eroding their constituencies, shedding particles which are carried by turbulent flows to reside at the bottom of sea beds. Tumultuous earth movements compress, bend and buckle these strata that have solidified into hard matter. Although explanations of the material residue of these spectacular events and more gradual processes often masquerade as dispassionate and scientific, they evoke fabulous scenarios of change that created the stony matter under inspection, bringing forth the recognition that cities are linked to unimaginably distant other times and places, and to processes taking millennia.

These geological temporalities pose fundamental questions about the stability and permanence of place. The Binney sandstone used in the initial construction of St Ann's was quarried at Collyhurst, one mile from the church, where in a local park, vestiges of the quarry face, abandoned over two hundred years ago remain. This stone is thus considered 'local' but in what sense can it be said to belong to Manchester? It may belong to the same ground on which Manchester is now sited but was not formed at the same latitude or longitude and neither was it part of the stable geological settlement of present times. This sandy matter was part of an arid desert which may have persisted for millennia but was then subjected to storms during which floods and torrents removed layers of sand and deposited them in oceans where the grains consolidated and solidified as rock. This reveals that, as Massey (2006: 35) claims, there is no 'intrinsic indigeneity' for 'both allegorically and materially … local place identity does not grow out of the soil.' Lynch's question – 'what time is this place?' – must take these pre-human temporalities into account to provide a fuller answer. Yet, the processes and events that occurred in these other times and places formed part of the material that has contributed to the character of central Manchester as it is now and has been over the past few centuries of human occupation.

Four of the most prevalent sandstones used in the construction of St Ann's provide in their embodiment a compendium of millennia spanning geological times. The aforementioned Binney stone is of Early Permian age, making it about 280 million years old, the yellow-grey Carboniferous stone extracted from the area around Darley Dale, Derbyshire, belongs to the millstone grit series of mid-Carboniferous times, making it about 320 million years ago, and the dark red Triassic Sherwood sandstone from Runcorn and the pinkish-white from Hollington in Staffordshire is roughly 230 years old.

The temporal scales of stone supply and uban connections

Geological time foregrounds the enormous temporal scales within which stone is embedded. We can further explore how a building 'is stitched into place by fragmented, multi-scaled and multi-sited networks of association' (Jacobs 2006: 3) to challenge reified and static conceptions of place. I now investigate the multiple connections of the stone at St Ann's to numerous other places to show how the church has been successively reconstituted by stone supplies from far and near, revealing the spatially diverse sources of stone and the temporalities that such connections evoke. This suggests an expanded time geography whereby the circulations, connections and routes of supply go beyond Hagerstrand's far more localized depiction of relations over short durations in which 'physical co-presence/absence and local connectedness are emphasized' but 'the conceptualization of relations at a distance is underdeveloped' (Schwanen 2007: 10).

Stone supply chains are provoked into being what Bruce Braun (2006: 647) calls 'imbroglios that mix together politics, machines, organisms, law, standards and grades, taste and aesthetics:' a range of factors including architectural fashion and style, building techniques, cost, technologies of transport and quarrying and stone masonry, and local politics in the sites of supply and destination. The successive historical connections to these supply sites and the subsequent importation of new and different building materials contribute to what Massey (1999) terms the 'mixity' of the city, further conjuring up the city's former constitution and the myriad connections that have now disappeared. Massey shows how numerous connections are manifest in the architectural remains of Mexico City as particular materials and buildings have been differentially enfolded into the city over time, producing different mixities as they change in appearance and texture, get demolished, modified, repaired and replaced, in single buildings and across the city as a whole. Building stone assembled in buildings and cities is thus constitutive of other places and times, of the histories of connections based on extraction and supply, and of the architectural and material echoes that resound between places. Similarly, the continual emergence of St Ann's Church as a material assemblage is an artefact through which we may identify the traces of the changing connections between places, their causes, and their geographical scale and duration (see Edensor and Drew 2007).

These material connections and assemblages may be stabilized for certain periods according to fashion, cost and availability, and the rate of decay, bonding people, technologies and places together for a while. Thus supply networks may be 'tightly coupled with complex, enduring, and predictable connections between peoples, objects, and technologies across multiple and distant spaces and times' (Sheller and Urry 2006: 216) while at other times they may be intermittent, volatile and variable. In Manchester, as with other cities, these flows have accelerated and expanded under conditions of rapid urban regeneration and growth (Edensor 2009), continuously transforming the material fabric of prosperous districts, although in less prosperous areas, ageing material fabric is patched up or left to decay.

In Manchester, building stone originally came from local sources, primarily Collyhurst, and then as the industrial revolution proceeded apace, and new canals and railways connected the city to places further afield, more supply sites were available. The development of the Peak Forest Canal made Derbyshire sandstones accessible, such as that quarried at Darley Dale. Later, more extensive, denser transport networks across the North-West and Midlands opened up other possibilities, including the Runcorn and Hollington Stone mentioned above. St Ann's embodies these successively exploited sites of stone supply. Because it was coated in black soot during the nineteenth century, it was not necessary to find replacement stone that matched the colour of the Collyhurst stone that had become eroded. Accordingly, the church is now a mosaic that testifies to the forging, disappearance and revival of such connections according to the taste for, and the economies and availabilities of particular sites of supply. The church has recently been further supplemented by red Triassic St Bees sandstone from Cumbria and mellow grey Kerridge sandstone from near Macclesfield in Cheshire.

The persistence or closure of these connections also impact upon and produce the temporal processes that occur in other places. The relationship between sites which demand stony matter and supply sites intimately determines the duration of extraction. Large scale quarrying at Darley Dale has ceased although smaller operations persist, Hollington remains an important source for the extraction for replacement stone and new buildings, while the massive Runcorn Quarry has been closed for over a hundred years and is now the site of a country park (see Edensor and Drew 2007). These temporal connections are also evident in what I refer to as interspatialities, where buildings from particular eras built out of locally quarried stone in the sites of supply resonate with those of a similar age in the place to which they were exported, undergirding Robert Sack's (2004: 248) claim that 'flows through space are the strands from places that are woven and re-woven to become elements in yet other places.' Certain prestigious stones and material that was produced in vast quantities at a particular time connect the histories of places. For instance, the deep red hues of Runcorn stone feature in a great diversity of structures including many buildings in Runcorn and its environs, other churches, schools and bridges in Manchester, Liverpool's Anglican cathedral, and New York and San Francisco docks (see 'A list of buildings containing Runcorn sandstone').

In present times, although older stone sources within the Midlands and North of England are still used to patch up the fabric of older buildings of Manchester, large building projects such as the large Arndale Shopping Centre extension and the recreational area of Spinningfields have imported granites, gabbro and marble from Italy, Brazil, China, Germany and South Africa (see Simpson and Broadhurst 2008; Edensor 2009). Stone supply networks have expanded over time and as new connections have been made, older relationships between places have evaporated.

In addition to the material temporalities marked by vanished, emergent and lasting connections between buildings and sites of supply, the building process also produces the 'superfluous landscapes' of the city, 'areas leftover from the planning and building of the city...that are not usable, not yet used, or already used and later abandoned' (Neilsen 2002: 54). These landscapes are not stable over time but are 'part of an ongoing transformation process on a material level' (Neilsen 2002: 56). Such mounds, pits and infills all evoke particular temporalities, and are often sited beyond the s boundaries of the city, which over time has reabsorbed them and reconfigured their usage, levelling them or perhaps turning them into wildlife reserves or parks. This reveals how the continuous emergence of the city in a more extensive time frame occurs through 'an interconnected series of processes (of) wasting, reappropriation and consumption of urban matter and space' (Neilsen 2002: 56).

The variable agencies of stone transformation

Stone may appear to be a solid entity but as I have insisted, it is continuously in the process of transformation and rearrangement. However, although stone has emergent qualities of its own, its life as coherent object also depends upon the temporal effects wrought by the host of agencies that invariably assail its integrity wherever it may come to reside as part of a building. These agencies are specific to place, are part of a distinct combination of flows and circulations that stream through, around and in place. Such agencies – climatic, plant, animal and chemical – settle and impact upon materiality in a host of different ways and work their destruction over multiple time frames; some effect stone rapidly over a very short spell, some work over very long periods, some are rhythmic, some intermittent and some dormant. Tim Ingold (2010: 2) accounts for these agencies in contending that 'materials of all sorts, with various and variable properties, and enlivened by the forces of the Cosmos, mix and meld with one another in the generation of things.' This ongoing (re)constitution of matter foregrounds 'an ontology that assigns primacy to processes of formation as against their final products, and to flows and transformations of materials as against states of matter,' so that stone and other matter are continuously in flux in its interaction and entanglement with other agents and processes, as part of a 'meshwork of interwoven lines of growth and movement (Ingold 2010: 3). These emergent qualities defy notions of material inviolability, and as Latham and McCormack's (2004) assert, the identification of such agents open up possibilities for exploring and 'apprehending different relations and durations of movement, speed and slowness' in the emergence of objects (Ingold 2004: 705). There are multiple agencies that impact upon the building stone of St Ann's at different rates and over varying periods, evoking various temporalities. Here, I focus upon the agencies of weather, iron and biofilms.

First, in Manchester, the temperate climate ensures regular rain, which along with wind and ice weakens building stone over time to greater effect than would be the case say, under Mediterranean conditions. Manchester's weather, although never wholly predictable, can be depicted as rhythmic in its seasonal effects, its monthly averages of rainfall and temperature, and by regular periods of wetting, drying and freezing, although there may be episodic periods of extreme weather. Despite this. however, localized, urban microclimatic processes make erosion somewhat uneven across the church's stone. The temporal cycles of erosion at St Ann's have generally had gradual effects upon stone, but this is speeded up in particular areas of the church, which have a greater propensity to collect water and freeze in harsh winters. Thus, rainwater collects in particular hollows and saturates the stone in the walls approximately 15 cm from the ground in the 'splash zones,' and around leaking gutters and pipes. According to the church's architect, the north-facing side has suffered more rapid erosion because it receives more direct rainfall, whereas other prospects are more sheltered by surrounding buildings. He also identifies 'some surface exfoliation which is a continuing problem' caused by weathering on the south and east elevations (Rank 2008: 6).

The impact of air pollution, through which the building was covered in the aforementioned black soot, was linked to the weather processes of the city, but the particularly baleful effects of sulphuric acid and nitrates in the acid rain, which resulted from the industrial smoke that dissolved the calcium carbonate within the stone of the church were arrested with the instituting of the Clean Air Acts of 1956 and 1968. However, although these severe causes of stone decay have declined, Wood et al. (1984: 60) estimate that in the mid-1980s, central Manchester levels of sulphur dioxide might increase the corrosion of stone by 50–70 per cent in comparison with surrounding rural areas and soiling by particulates added 10–25 per cent to cleaning costs.

Secondly, these more rhythmic although uneven climatic processes that impact upon the durability of stone co-exist with more latent agencies that may suddenly explode into action after many years. A good example of this agential temporality at St Ann's is the presence of iron staples that were inserted beneath the stone many years ago. They secured the building for a while but as stone weathered and weakened over time, it cracked and allowed water to seep through to reach the iron beneath. What had been stable was suddenly catalysed by this moisture and the iron began to rust, expanding in the process and causing the surrounding stones to fracture. This highlights how certain agencies may become volatile after remaining dormant for centuries. Stability may turn to instability with attendant consequences for surrounding material.

Thirdly, there are the complex biological temporalities of biofilms, single or multi-species populations of micro-organisms that can adhere to each other and colonize stone surfaces (Cezar, Gaylarde and Gaylarde 2002). Biofilms contain complex consortia of algae, cyanobacteria, heterotrophic bacteria, fungi, lichens, protozoa and a variety of small animals, mosses and plants and depend on many different conditions, such as the properties and capacities of the stone they colonize. Biofilms can cause damage to stone, releasing destructive acids and penetrative endolithic micro-organisms, exploiting structural irregularities of stone for their growth, notably moist fissures. To prosper, they require nutrients and moisture, a porous surface and an alkalinity below pH 8, conditions present in the stone of St Ann's where these green forms are evident in areas where rainwater pools and drips, and on and around ledges, leaking gutters and pipes, and in the splash zones. In drier parts of the church, the biofilm is less evident. The current architect, Rank (2008) regards the biofilms as currently unthreatening although he warns that they may become damaging if left unattended over time. However, although colonization is rarely harmful to start with, where conditions are suitable, biofilms grow stronger and denser, drawing more organisms into their community. When they reach this point they rapidly start to erode the stone. The biofilm's potential growth into a community will impact upon the security of the stone. This is a temporality that is not slow and inexorable but is characterized by slow development followed by rapid erosive power after having little impact.

The agencies discussed above are of varying temporal scale. The earlier effects of air pollution swirling around Greater Manchester have now disappeared though unpredictable forms of air pollution persist. The agencies of internal metal are catalysed in and around the fabric of the church and become active like the biofilms, which, following periods of growth, can cause damage over a short period. Both agents might be depicted as timebombs. But these temporalities also resonate with Bergson's (2001) ideas of becoming as ongoing continuum – here, the endless becoming of things. And there is rhythm too – never absolute repetition – but the rhythm of the seasons, off the cycles of growth and decay and of the systematic human endeavours to secure the mirage of material stability and separateness, as I now discuss.

Illusions of permanence and endurance: The rhythms of repair

The depredations upon stone of numerous non-human agencies reveal the fragility and evanescence of building materials and the structures to which they belong. Dewsbury (2000: 487) asks, 'The building you walk through/within – what is the speed of flux that is keeping it assembled?' and answers, 'It seems permanent…but it is ephemeral nonetheless: whilst you are there it is falling down, it is just happening very slowly (hopefully).' This disassembly may seem slow given its relationship to the contrasting temporalities of the human life span but it depends upon the (changing) local agencies, the properties and capacities of the materials, and their suitability to the (changing) environment to which they are moved. Yet, however, relatively durable stone may be, Smith emphasizes the futility of expecting buildings to endure: 'whoever expects to find a stone that will stand from century to century, deriding alike the frigid rains and scorching solar rays, without need of reparation, will indeed search for the philosopher's stone' (Smith 1842, quoted in Bristow 1998). So it is that strategies to maintain structures, to restore their material integrity, rely upon the institutionalized practices of repair.

The effects of the non-human agents of destruction discussed above mean that unless remedial action is taken, the materiality of a building will turn to ruin and eventually dust (Edensor 2005a). Thus, 'a sense of foundation and stable locatedness' (Massey 2006: 34) albeit for particular time periods only, provides what Jacobs (2006: 3) calls the 'coherent given-ness' of a building to secure an illusion of material fixity. I have already discussed the supply of additional stone to replace eroded matter as a means to perpetuate the life of buildings. Linked to this process are the procedures of repair and maintenance. We might characterize such practices as emblematic of the regular, rhythmic endeavours through which the city is continuously restored at various scales, whether daily, weekly or over longer time spells, as part of the 'polyrhythmic ensemble' (Crang 2001) that characterizes place. As Lefebvre (2004: 15) asserts, 'everywhere where there is interaction between a place, a time, and an expenditure of energy, there is rhythm,' the regular repetition of movements and action, the particular entanglements of linear and cyclical rhythms that offer a consistency to place over time. Yet as Lefebvre also declares, 'there is nothing inert in the world,' referring to the often unrecognized rhythmic processes of the non-human, some of which are identified above. It is to combat the effects of these destructive rhythms that the instrumental rhythms of repair are institutionalized.

St Ann's, like all Anglican churches, is presently legally required to undergo a quinquennial inspection by a qualified architect. Thus, rhythmic process of inspection is more exactly timed in comparison with the maintenance procedures of earlier times. Nevertheless, there is a compendium of traces showing interventions into the stone of St Ann's, a veritable catalogue of successive material amendments, additions, removals and treatments that have tried to ensure that it 'perdures' over time (Tait and While 2009). The enrolment of technologies through routine human practices produces rhythmic stabilities (Schwanen 2007: 12). Thus, a battery of maintenance techniques have been used at St Ann's over the past three centuries. Brushing, washing and steaming have been used to remove biofilms and the soot that once coated the building, although the church has been spared the baleful effects of the overuse of abrasive techniques of cleansing because gentler cleansing solutions have been used. Yet, the application of rendering on the church to replace worn mortar and stone is extremely variable. Some mortar is very hard, some soft, some coloured and textured to fit in with the adjacent stone and some of different hue. Some infills have been crudely applied but elsewhere are neat. In several areas, the stone has crumbled at the edges because impermeable mortar has diverted moisture to the back of the stone and it has decayed from within. More recent mortar repairs use a permeable lime mixture, which has not produced the damaging earlier consequences. Apart from evident recent interventions, the age of most of these myriad attempts at repair traced across the stone fabric of the church are of indeterminate age, but they all testify to an ongoing effort to ensure that St Ann's remains an enduring fixture in central Manchester.

The enormous variety of these techniques, approaches and applications demonstrates that although Lefebvre (2004: 6) insists that there is no 'rhythm without repetition in time and space, without reprises, without returns, in short, without measure,' he is also insistent that 'there is no identical absolute repetition indefinitely…there is always something new and unforeseen that introduces itself into the repetitive.' Accordingly, although a regular occurrence, repair contingently addresses immediate circumstances, for 'improvisation is key since fault-finding and repair is a process of ongoing, situated enquiry' (Graham and Thrift 2007: 7), a contingent endeavour, using continually changing techniques and technologies and having to take into account shifting materialities, social and environmental conditions, particular agencies, and aesthetics. Repair is thus not characterized by seamless technical progress but by an abundance of contested views and a history of abandoned techniques. This accords with Simpson's (2008: 810) claim that rhythm provides a backdrop to life against which the usual and the unusual unfold, against which practice is reproduced and improvised, (re)producing 'a stable but also evental everyday temporality' replete with 'different durations with concomitant durabilities,' characterized by immanent and emergent possibilities in addition to repetitive rhythms.

Ghostly traces and the forgotten

The multi-temporal materiality of St Ann's inadvertently honours the interwoven histories of the non-human agencies in the composition of place, the rise and fall of stone supply connections that drew places and people together, and those who have successively secured the materiality of the church against erasure. This particular place exemplifies how all urban space is invariably 'a palimpsest composed of different temporal elements, featuring signs, objects and vaguer traces that rebuke the tendencies to move on and forget' (Edensor 2008: 313), though this is more obscure in some spaces than others.

Michel de Certeau (1984: 108) claims that places are 'haunted by many different spirits, spirits one can "invoke" or not', and that 'haunted places are the only ones people can live in.' Here, the church is vividly haunted by a profusion of non-human and human agents from different times, and especially the quarrymen, transport workers, masons, repairers and artisans that are 'absolutely essential and yet never fully acknowledged' (Harvey 2010: 357), those 'people who are primarily unseen and banished to the periphery of our social graciousness' (Gordon 1997: 196). Here, these material traces of revenant time often obscure vestiges that can rebuke attempts to produce smooth, linear and exclusionary historical narratives about places (Edensor 2005b).

As I have argued, although repair leaves a compendium of traces of different interventions on a building's materiality, it also purports to arrest time by maintaining a continuous physical presence and coherence in the wake of the innumerable destructive energies that circulate around and upon a building. This raises questions about the desirability of endlessly securing sites of material assemblage in the face of constant change. Caitlin DeSilvey (2011) discusses how the cost of endlessly repairing the renowned picturesque harbour at Mullion Cove, Cornwall in response to its regular erosion by the sea has culminated in a decision by the National Trust, who own the site, to begin a policy of managed retreat. For DeSilvey (2011), the harbour is 'a temporary arrangement of matter, made durable by a twentieth-century heritage discourse that granted it a symbolic cultural value' but she calls for an anticipatory history that is not predicated on the certainty of the unfolding past of a place but instead acknowledges its contingencies, discontinuities and multiplicities in how it has come to be, and thus she contends that we should read creativity 'forwards,' as an improvisatory joining in with formative processes, rather than 'backwards,' as if we are confronting a finished entity.

At St Ann's, the endless transformation of matter and the numerous decisions that have been made to secure the building raise other questions about how the church should be conserved. St Ann's is unusual in that its very composition exposes the constant modifications and interventions it has continuously undergone, and so there is no possibility of preserving some pristine simulacra of the original building. It is a vivid material compendium of different social and non-human agencies over three centuries. Because the surface is multicoloured – red white, yellow and purple – decisions have to be made about which stone should be used to replace eroded material? The oldest material, the Collyhurst stone is no longer quarried and is friable.

Aesthetic questions of restoration and conservation are raised by this evident multi-temporality. How might future interventions accommodate and respond to further change? By going back to some sort of imagined original design? By carefully reproducing a material mixity in harmony with the presently existing mosaic? Or by introducing new materials, textures and colours into the building with the surety that these too will meld and deteriorate in a particular and unpredictable ways? What in the end will be materially original in the church other than its basic shape, function and position? In fact, like Leonardo's *Last Supper*, is it already a pale echo of what existed once upon a time, the catalogue of innumerable interventions into its ever-transforming materiality making a ghost of the early eighteenth century building?

References

Adam, Barbara (1998), *Timescapes of Modernity*, London: Routledge.

Bennett, Jane (2008), 'A life, of men and metal', Conference Paper, Annual Meeting of the Association of American Geographers, Boston, USA

Bergson, Henri (2001), *Time and Free Will: An Essay on the Immediate Data of Consciousness*, London: Dover Books.

Braun, Bruce (2006), 'Environmental issues: global natures in the space of assemblage', *Progress in Human Geography*, 30: 5, pp. 644–654.

Bristow, Ian (1998), 'An introduction to the restoration, conservation and repair of stone', in Ashurst, J. and Dimes, F. (eds), *Conservation of Building and Decorative Stone*, Oxford: Butterworth Heineman.

Bouzarovski, Stephan (2009), 'Building Events in Inner-City Gdansk, Poland: Exploring the Sociospatial Construction of Agency in Built Form', *Environment and Planning D: Society and Space*, 27, pp. 840–858.

Boyer, Christine (1996), *The City of Collective Memory*, Cambridge, MA: MIT Press.

Cezar, Crispim; Gaylarde, Peter and Gaylarde, Christine (2002) 'Algal and Cyanobacterial Biofilms on Calcareous Historic Buildings', *Current Microbiology*, 46: 2, pp. 79–82.

Crang, Mike (2001), 'Rhythms of the city: temporalised space and motion', in Jon May and Nigel Thrift (eds), *Timespace: Geographies of Temporality*, London: Routledge, pp.187-207.

Crang, Mike and Travlou, Penny (2001), 'The City and Topologies of Memory', *Environment and Planning D: Society and Space*, 19, pp. 161–177.

De Certeau, Michel (1984), *The Practice of Everyday Life*, Berkeley: University of California Press.

DeSilvey, Caitlin (2011), 'Making Sense of Transience: An Anticipatory History', *Cultural Geographies* (forthcoming).

Dewsbury, J.D. (2000), 'Performativity and the Event: Enacting a Philosophy of Difference', *Environment and Planning D: Society and Space* 18, pp. 473–496.

Dodgson, Robert (2008), 'Geography's Place in Time', *Geografiska Annaler*, 90: 1, pp. 1–15.

Edensor, Tim (2005a), 'Waste Matter: The Debris of Industrial Ruins and the Disordering of the Material World', *Journal of Material Culture*, 10: 3, pp. 311–322.

Edensor, Tim (2005b), 'The Ghosts of Industrial Ruins: Ordering and Disordering Memory in Excessive Space', *Environment and Planning D: Society and Space*, 23, pp. 829–849.

Edensor, Tim and Drew, Ian (2007), 'Building Stone in the City of Manchester', http://www.sci-eng.mmu.ac.uk/manchester_stone/. 11.11.10.

Edensor, Tim (2008), 'Mundane Hauntings: Commuting Through the Phantasmagoric Working Class Spaces of Manchester, England', *Cultural Geographies* 15, pp. 313–333.

Edensor, Tim (2009), 'Building stone in Manchester: networks of materiality, circulating matter and the ongoing constitution of the city', in Michael Guggenheim and Ola Söderström (eds), *Re-Shaping Cities*, London: Routledge, pp. 211-230.

Gordon, Avery (1997), *Ghostly Matters*, Minneapolis: Minnesota University Press.

Graham, Steven and Thrift, Nigel (2007), 'Out of Order: Understanding Repair and Maintenance', *Theory, Culture & Society*, 24: 3, pp. 1–25.

Harvey, David (2010), 'Broad Down, Devon: Archaeological and Other Stories', *Journal of Material Culture*, 15: 3, pp. 345–367.

Hurcombe, Linda (2007), *Archaeological Artefacts as Material Culture*, London: Routledge.

Ingold, Tim (2004), 'Buildings', in Stephan Harrison, Steve Pile and Nigel Thrift (eds), *Patterned Ground: Entanglements of Nature and Culture*, London: Reaktion, pp. 238-240.

Ingold, Tim (2010), *Working Paper #15: Bringing Things to Life: Creative Entanglements in a World of Materials*, http://www.socialsciences.manchester.ac.uk/realities/publications/workingpapers/15-2010-07-realities-bringing-things-to-life.pdf, 11.11.10.

Ingold, Tim and Hallam, Elizabeth (2007), 'Creativity and cultural improvisation: an introduction', in Elizabethy Hallam and Tim Ingold (eds), *Creativity and Cultural Improvisation*, Oxford: Berg, pp. 1-24.

Jacobs, Jane (2006), 'A geography of big things', *Cultural Geographies*, 1, pp. 1–27.

Latham, Alan and McCormack, Derek (2004), 'Moving Cities: Rethinking the Materialities of Urban Geographies', *Progress in Human Geography*, 28: 6, pp. 701–724.

Lefebvre, Henri (2004), *Rhythmanalysis: Space, Time and Everyday Life*, London: Continuum.

Lynch, Kevin (1972), *What Time is this Place?*, Cambridge, MA: MIT Press.

Massey, Doreen (1999), 'Cities in the world', in Doreen Massey, John Allen and Steve Pile (eds), *City Worlds*, London: Routledge, pp. 95-156.

Massey, Doreen (2006), 'Landscape as a Provocation: Reflections on Moving Mountains', *Journal of Material Culture*, 11: 1/2, pp. 33–48.

May, Jon and Thrift, Nigel (eds) (2001), 'Introduction' in Jon May and Nigel Thrift (eds), *Timespace: Geographies of Temporality*, London: Routledge, pp. 1-46.

Neilsen, Tom (2002) 'The Return of the Excessive: Superfluous Landscapes', *Space and Culture*, 5: 1, pp. 53–62.

Rank, Nicholas (2008), *Quinquennial Inspection Report for St Ann's Church, Diocese of Manchester, Deanery of Hulme*, Buttress, Fuller, Alsop and Williams Architects, Manchester.

Runcorn and District Historical Society, 'A list of buildings containing Runcorn sandstone', http://www.runcornhistsoc.org.uk/buildings_runcorn_stone.html. Accessed July 2009.

Sack, Robert (2004), 'Place-making and time', in Tom Mels (ed.), *Reanimating Places: A Geography of Rhythms*, Aldershot: Ashgate, pp. 243-254.

St Ann's Manchester, http://www.stannsmanchester.com/content/view/133/141/, 11.11.10.

Schwanen, Tim (2007), 'Matter(s) of interest: artefacts, spacing and timing', *Geografiska Annaler*, 89 B: 1, pp. 9–22.

Sheller, Mimi and Urry, John (2006) 'The New Mobilities Paradigm', *Environment and Planning A*, 38, pp. 207–226.

Simpson, Ian and Broadhurst, Fred (2008), *A Building Stones Guide to Central Manchester*, 2nd edn, Manchester: Manchester Geological Association.

Simpson, Paul (2008), 'Chronic Everyday Life: Rhythmanalysing Street Performance', *Social and Cultural Geography*, 9: 7, pp. 807–829.

Tait, Malcolm and While, Aidan (2009), 'Ontology and the Conservation of Built Heritage', *Environment and Planning D: Society and Space*, 27, pp. 721–737.

Winkler, Erhard (1994), *Stone in Architecture: Properties, Durability*, London: Springer-Verlag.

Wood, C., Lee, N., Luker, J. and Saunders, P. (1984), *The Geography of Pollution: A Study of Greater Manchester*, Manchester: Manchester University Press.

Yussof, Kathryn and Gabrys, Jennifer (2006), 'Time Lapses: Robert Smithson's Mobile Landscapes', *Cultural Geographies*, 32, pp. 444–450.

Part II

Relational Configurations

Chapter 4

Shifting Topographies: Sound and *The Fragmented Orchestra*

Jane Grant and John Matthias

The Fragmented Orchestra combines conceptually simple but technically precise elements (microphone, speaker, communicator and 'neuron') into an elegant, geographically distributed network structure. The result is a vast musical brain, which promises to generate pieces that touch upon extraordinarily disparate aspects of music and culture, such as audience participation, sampling as instrument, endogenous composition, aesthetics of technology, and more. Among the most intriguing of these many resonances is the way in which *The Fragmented Orchestra* establishes an audible analogy between the brain and the internet, such that the music produced becomes an artefact of their parallel structures. This composition renders in sound the sense in which the internet is already a singular mind, the collective compositional creativity of the crowd singing in one voice.

Aden Evens (2008), author of *Sound Ideas Music,
Machines, and Experience* (2005)

The Fragmented Orchestra by Jane Grant, John Matthias and Nick Ryan was installed in the United Kingdom between December 2008 and February 2009. It consisted of 24 fixed geographical locations, such as FACT, Liverpool; University of Plymouth; Landscove Primary School, Devon; The National Portrait Gallery, London; Millennium Stadium, Cardiff and Kielder Observatory, Northumberland. At each of the locations, a 'soundbox' was installed, which consisted of a microphone, a small computer connected to the internet and a Feonic 'drive', a device that transmits audio through resonating architectural surfaces. Sound made in the spaces was transmitted across the internet as mp3 compressed audio, to a server computer in the FACT gallery using code written by Daniel Jones (Jones et al. 2009). In this computer, we continually ran an artificial neuronal network, an adaptation of the recently developed Izhikevich's non-linear integrate and fire model (Izhikevich et al. 2004) that incorporates spatial 'axonal delays' between synapses (junctions between neurons) and a spike-timing-dependent plasticity (STDP) algorithm, which causes the synaptic strengths between neurons to become updated as a function of the differences in signal arrival times. This code, written by Tim Hodgson (Jones et al. 2009), was configured into two audio units, one of which contained 24 artificial neurons (a tiny 'cortex'), each of which was stimulated by a single channel of the incoming audio signals to the server. The other audio unit contained a 'granulation' algorithm that configured the incoming audio into sound grains, which were triggered at the neuronal firing times.

Each of the 24 channels of generated audio was sent to a loudspeaker hanging in Gallery 1 at FACT. The 24 suspended speakers relayed the neuronally triggered sounds from each individual site. The audience, weaving their way through the space, was able to hear the live composition as a whole and listen to each of the sites individually. Occasionally, huge sonic 'waves' filled the gallery with sound, whereas at other times, smaller, more discreet events occurred which had to be listened to more intently. The geographic frame is reordered and miniaturized within the gallery, allowing the listeners to compose

Figure 1. *The Fragmented Orchestra*, installation view.

the work as they move around the space, the final composition of this geographically extended work occurring in the brain/ear of the listener. The streamed sound from all of the 24 locations combined at the gallery was also sent back through the internet to each of the sites and played through the Feonic drive, where the public, invited to 'play' the instrument, was able to hear the effect that its playing had on the overall composition of the piece. We designed an interface on the website (www.thefragmentedorchestra.com) where listeners could compose on *The Fragmented Orchestra* with either separate site elements, combinations of sites or by listening to the evolving composition as a whole.

Hourly, daily, weekly and monthly time scales at the sites were all re-composed in real time by the neuronal instrument. Many time scales – the vast and the miniscule – merged in the gallery and the cortex changed and adapted its behaviour according to the stimulation it received. The neurons stimulated each other to fire, occasionally resulting in a collective pulsing from all 24 locations.

The geographical locations for *The Fragmented Orchestra* were chosen in two ways: one by invitation and the other by proactive research. In May 2008, the composers – Jane Grant, John Matthias and Nick Ryan – the PRS Foundation and FACT emailed thousands of people and institutions inviting them to propose a location to be considered as one of the 24 sites. They were asked to describe in 100 words why their site was sonically interesting. The response was impressive, with proposals coming in from all over the United Kingdom including evocative descriptions of sounds and locations. The final 24 sites were chosen for their inherent sonic rhythms, their geographical location and the significance and function of the site.

Brain and geographical space

The specifics of how neurons with intrinsic firing time scales in the millisecond range can give rise to thoughts that may last for a number of seconds is enticing both scientifically and philosophically (Hopfield and Brody 2001). These time scales, ranging from milliseconds to seconds have an intrinsic spatial aspect, a temporal wave across minute topologies. There are approximately one hundred thousand million neurons (or nerve cells) in the human brain and each of these neurons connects to approximately 10,000 others. Some of these neurons are *sensory* neurons, directly connected to the outside world and some of them are *motor* neurons and perform a function of making our bodies move and react. Many of the neurons are simply concerned with processing information coming in from sensory neurons and are *cortical* neurons located in the cerebral cortex, a sheet of neural tissue the size of France, which is folded up around the cerebrum of the mammalian brain. Each of these neurons has a cellular membrane that has a resting potential difference, a small voltage of about 65 mV, across it (roughly 500 times smaller than the voltage from an average household battery). When a neuron gets stimulated electrically (either from the outside world, if it is a sensory neuron or from signals from other neurons), and the membrane voltage gets higher than a certain threshold level, it will fire a signal to all the neurons to which it is connected. This signal takes the form of a 'spike' of voltage, a very short signal which has a duration of around 1 ms.

This 'spiking' behaviour is mediated by the flow of electrical ions in and out of the cellular membrane and was first understood in detail by the mathematical biologists Alan Hodgkin and Andrew Huxley who, in the early 1950s, combined detailed electrical experiments with the axon of a giant squid in Plymouth, England with mathematical calculations on one of the earliest computers, an EDSAC machine in Cambridge. The theory of the 'Action Potential' or the Hodgkin–Huxley model as it is also known, is still the best theory we have of neuronal spiking behaviour.

Although the Hodgkin–Huxley theory is an excellent theory, it is unwieldy, computationally very expensive and very difficult to implement for networks of neurons. Physicists have therefore tended to use simplified versions of the Hodgkin–Huxley theory to try and understand emergent properties of network behaviour, not predictable by using a single neuron model. How one simplifies a theory is partly dependent on the particular problem which the mathematical physicist wants to solve; a physicist will tend to throw out parts of the theory which they feel might be irrelevant for the job in hand. Often, spatial and topological concerns have been the parts which physicists have neglected when modelling neuronal spiking behaviour, as their concerns have been largely temporal. It has only been in the last five years or so that we have seen a leap in the understanding of the crucial and delicate spatial–temporal relationships within neural networks in mainstream computational neuroscience. We have included three of these major new and inter-related spatio-temporal considerations in the modelling of the neuronal network in *The Fragmented Orchestra*: Polychronisation, STDP and axonal conduction delays.

Polychronization is an idea which considers that a stimulated cell will cause a cluster of firing activity among a subset of connected cells, which will fire at subsequent times determined by the distances of the connected cells and their current state. This spatio-temporal set of information in the firing group is, in some sense, mapped to the sensual information that triggered the firing of the initially stimulated cell. Other sensual triggers will cause different neurons in the connected ensemble to fire. It is therefore the combination of possible 'firings' in the ensemble of neurons, which give the brain its huge processing power, a number that is related to both the number of neurons and the topology of firing groups. The number of such groups of neurons in brain circuits has been estimated as being larger than the number of elementary particles in the whole Universe. Izhikevich et al. (2004) also consider that this model forms a very simple form of memory, in which the re-triggering of the spatio-temporal firing set by the brain conjures up the initial sensual trigger. In this picture, it is the temporal and topological pattern of firing across large groups of neurons that form the link between sensing and the action and back to the virtual sense in terms of memorial trigger.

The presence of both STDP and axonal conduction delays are crucial for polychronization. Axons are the long cellular tubes that connect a cell body to synapses and spike signals have a finite velocity along them. Axonal conduction delays are a way of modelling the delay caused by the travel duration of the spike signal along the axon. In infancy, the human brain forms a map of the body in relation to itself and movement in external space. However, this map, or more accurately, topology, is mutable in relation to the body's position in space. The body/brain continually adapts and updates its relation to space and also to extensions of the body, in the use of tools for example. One of the ways in which the brain adapts itself is known as 'plasticity'. This has been divided into two possibly distinct, but undoubtedly related effects, known as 'structural' and 'synaptic' plasticity. 'Structural' plasticity concerns the changing of the cellular rewiring in the brain. New sensual experiences can cause new synapses (junctions) to form between neurons that are continually growing axons from the cell bodies. These axons are driven to grow towards rapidly firing cells (across a chemical gradient) and form new synapses, in a process which is known as 'Synaptogenesis'. This new circuitry is transient and its robustness depends on the future utilization of the new junctions; and the synapses will die away if they become redundant (Goda 2003).

'Synaptic Plasticity' refers to the adaptation of the strengths of connections between neurons in the cerebral cortex. Typically, a connection will be increased if a pre-synaptic neuron causes a post-synaptic neuron to fire. The connection is depressed if the firing of the post-synaptic neuron occurs before the pre-synaptic neuron has fired, a phenomenon known as 'spike-timing dependent plasticity'. The time scale of the structural plasticity is thought to be hours or days, whereas the synaptic plasticity has time scales that range over numbers of seconds. The combination of the axonal conduction delays, the STDP and the stimulation of the neuronal network from the public sites 'polychronises' *The Fragmented Orchestra*. It enables sites to emerge in clusters, activating each other to become audible in the central space and across the network, evolving spatio-temporal waves.

Sound and synapses – movement and thought

A synapse is a gap, an absence of tangible matter, a space of formation in the state of becoming. The synapse is a place where information exists but is unformed and is still in the process of its own conclusion. There are interesting analogies between the flow of information across the cortex and the connectivity of the sites across *The Fragmented Orchestra*. Although all sounds were continuously streamed from each of the 24 locations, the only sonic information heard was that which occurred when the 'neurons' fired. These clusters of firing neurons build architectures of time, not matter, each event forming a new time-based 'space' within the system. *The Fragmented Orchestra* highlights both the minute spaces of the brain and the 'event space' of the networked work of art. Although physically smaller but enormously more intricate, the functioning cortex is built of an infinitesimal series of complex events. These events are not structures of matter but structures of time, the result of established pathways, new sensory input and noise in the system. As an artwork, *The Fragmented Orchestra* covered a vast area of physical space, a network across the United Kingdom. However, the work did not exist in any 'space' at all. Although there were 24 connected sites and a central exhibition area, the real 'space' of the work was in the connectivity of the sites, the in-between, in the temporal firing events of the work. All that was evident regarding the materials of the work were speakers, 'soundboxes', wires, microphones and a central 'listening space'. The invisible structure that allowed these events to be networked, to communicate, was the internet. Sound in this instance is interesting because it has the ability to create a space without a tangible physical presence, echoing the clusters of firing neurons in Izhikevich's model. Moreover, these fleeting sonic events were unrecorded, only existing in the time it took to hear them.

Self and boundaries

In his book *Consciousness Explained*, Daniel C. Dennett (1991) proposes the notion of the 'self' as a construction: a 'naïve boundary between 'me' and 'the outside world'. Even such a simple self is not a concrete thing but just an abstraction, a principle of organization. The boundaries of a biological self are porous and indefinite. Philosophically speaking, current work in the field of phenomenology and in particular, that of David Wood (2000) in his essay, 'Time shelters: an essay in the poetics of time' (Durie and Webb 2000) argues that boundaries are interchangeable as states, that 'a boundary is not a thing, but a cluster of procedures for the management of otherness'. This 'cluster of procedures' and the concept of the porosity of the boundaries of the self are significant in relation to *The Fragmented Orchestra*. Neuronal research, observation of activity alongside the creation of models, brings about many philosophical questions. Neuroscience, although still in its infancy, is beginning to modify some of the most basic ideas regarding who we are. Physical and mathematical research into the configuration, adaptability and functionality of the brain conflict and sometimes conflate with fundamental questions on the nature of the self. The neuropsychologist, Paul Broks considers that there is no self in the matter of the human brain: it is a creation within the construction of the human brain and in the connectivity of groups of firing neurons and chemical release (Broks 2003). It could be said that human consciousness does not reside in matter but does reside in time, in the clusters of firing neurons, growing and adapting according to sensory input and noise in the system.

Developmental work

The motivation of the early part of the research which eventually formed *The Fragmented Orchestra* concerned the evolution of the neuronal firing patterns in the temporal domain. When modelling neuronal activity on a computer, neuroscientists often use a 'raster plot' – a plot of neuronal firing activity across time. Typically, we might see a group of 1000 neurons pictured on the ordinate axis of a graph, with time plotted on the abscissa. When a neuron 'fires,' a dot is placed in line with the firing neuron at a co-ordinate commensurate with

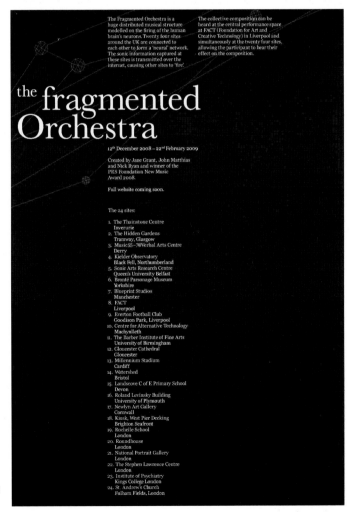

Figure 2. The 24 sites of *The Fragmented Orchestra*.

the firing time, and the whole graph displays a collective picture of temporal firing activity. Although the firing times of the neurons in these model simulations are indeterminate, they nevertheless produce correlated and structured patterns on a raster plot. Random firing times would produce a raster plot without pattern or structure. We began to consider the idea that the firing time (or 'dot' on the raster plot) could be mapped directly to a 'sonic event' and we constructed a prototype instrument with Eduardo Miranda and Tim Hodgson, which we called the 'Neurogranular sampler' in which a grain of sound (which had a duration typically of 50 ms) was selected and triggered from a recorded sound file in the computer when one of the model neurons fired (Grant et al. 2009).

Early versions of the sampler appeared to create time patterns and rhythms that destabilized temporal aural expectation. These 'internal' neurological rhythms appear unfamiliar to us. They are liminal, existing at the boundary or threshold of what might be perceived as an internal rhythm. The 'granular' element within the instrument also introduces a sensual boundary; below a duration of around 20 ms, all sounds are perceived as 'clicks' and it is impossible for us to distinguish the frequencies of the sound sources. The introduction of the firing event with a sonic event or 'action' circumvents any 'motor' action that we would expect to occur in a real brain/body in which a sense precedes processing which causes action. In the Neurogranular sampler, the motor action *is* the processing and the processing re-triggers the sensual input, which is temporally re-configured. Experiments with the sampler resulted in an exploration of the temporal domain, by elongating and shortening grain sizes and we began to introduce the spatial by introducing synaptic plasticity and axonal delays into the computer model. This enabled the instrument's output to adapt and change according to the adapting strengths of connections between the artificial neurons and introduced the internal adapting neuronal group topology.

Scales and topography

There has been much written about temporal concerns in music. Stockhausen's (1959) famous essay '... how time passes ...' attempted to remove barriers between rhythm and pitch, partly preserved for the purposes of serial composition (when you speed up rhythm, it enters the pitch domain). More recently, Curtis Roads (2004) considers temporal scales in music ranging from the granular threshold we have already mentioned, through the duration of musical phrases and movements and up to the duration of stylistic changes over decades and centuries. Almost all of this writing regards music as a sequence of notes 'moving through time' and seemingly disregards the spatial. It is as though the music simply exists on a score or within a recording and that rooms, walls, performers and public interaction are at best, secondary and at worst, irrelevant. Introducing spatial concerns also introduces the topologies, complexities and the fluctuations of spatial interaction, which are disregarded in a 'mean-field' description of scale.

The Fragmented Orchestra highlights the mutually co-existing and co-dependent temporal and spatial scales at millisecond (tenths of millimetres), second (metres to miles), daily, weekly and monthly (feet and miles) scales. At all of these temporal and spatial scales, patterns and topologies emerge through several levels of self-organization across neuronal, internet and social networks, which give *The Fragmented Orchestra* its sound. The temporal evolution of the sound is inextricably linked to the emergence of the spatio-temporal dynamic on all of these networks. The time patterns of everyday life – night to day, silence to noise, work to sleep – are entangled with the topology of consciousness.

Thresholds and topology

The neuron connected to each site will fire if the volume of sound into the microphone exceeds a certain threshold value, the neuron can also be made to fire from pre-synaptic signals from other neurons and also from a global uncorrelated network 'noise' that simulates global brain activity external to the micro-cortex (Izhikevich 2004). The topology of connectivity of the neuronal network was 'all-to-all' that is much more strongly connected than real neurons in the mammalian cortex, which typically connect with around 10 per cent of the other cortical neurons. This 'all-to-all' connection topology meant that the geographical sites were also connected to each other, which removes any local relational geographical topology.

The patterns of firing, and therefore the temporal evolution of the sound on *The Fragmented Orchestra* rely upon delicate dynamic relationships between the volume of the externally stimulating sound, the evolution of the plasticity algorithm that continually updates the connectivity of the neuronal network and the timing of the arrival signals from other neurons. The combination of these effects renders the formation of transient polychronous groups across the multi-speaker installation in the main gallery. Relationships between sites affected by the neuronal interaction can be heard as repeated rhythms and patterns across the speakers in the central space. These relationships are transient and appear to develop but then disappear, to be replaced by different patterns and rhythms. Spatial and temporal relationships between speakers, sites and sound remain unfixed. In the gallery space, there is a scale transference from the spatial and geographical, to the minute and model biological back into a spatial representation in a gallery. Phenomenologically, there is a tension between these scales or spaces of perception.

The analogies between the flow of information across the cortex, the relationship between dynamics of individual firing neurons and emerging firing group structures in the network, and the idea of a crowd at a sports match having multiple parts forming a whole, were at the core of the decision to choose Everton Football Club and Millennium Stadium as sites for *The Fragmented Orchestra*. The regular stimulation from one site (e.g.

during the England–Wales rugby match at Millennium Stadium) affects the 'cortex' as a whole, continually stimulating all the other neurons (because of the all-to-all connection topology) and increasing the overall sound level in *The Fragmented Orchestra* for the duration of games at the stadia. The idea of 'fluid' sound coming from the games being fragmented and overlaid became very intriguing; minute ripples and changes of sound, pensiveness mixed with expectation. With speech there are gaps and pauses, whereas with tens of thousands of people all shouting and singing together you cannot hear the gaps, just a huge wave of sound. The continuous wave collected and overlaid sections of the sound, allowing a build up of sonic phrases gently cancelling each other out.

Passivity to agency

The Fragmented Orchestra cannot generate new sounds. The noise in the system keeps the model buoyant and allows the model to self generate events from previous stimuli (Grant 2010). The neurons in *The Fragmented Orchestra* have both a sensory and cortical character in the sense that they are all connected to the outside world and all function as processing agents. Because of this and the fact that the system as a whole is being continually stimulated, some of the longer-term dynamics such as pulsing were rarely seen in the 2008–09 installation. Because the system was being continually stimulated, the relationship between the long-term 'learning' and the 'short-term' stimulation was difficult to track. This is where a shift from passivity to agency occurs. The agency within the work lies predominantly with the listener/player, in participation with the system. This allows complexity and play, where listeners become active players. Any 'intelligence' resides in the human participation rather than in the neuronal modelling or network. However, the authorship of the work does not lie with either party; time patterns, rhythms, volume and pitch are all dependant on the complexity of the structure of active and passive parties whether human or computer modelled.

References

Broks, P. (2004), *Into the Silent Land: Travels in Neuropsychology*, New York and London: Grove Press.

Dennett, D.C. (1991), *Consciousness Explained*, London: Penguin.

Evens, A. (2005), *Sound Ideas: Music, Machines and Experience*, Minneapolis, MN: University of Minnesota Press.

Evens, A. (2008), www.thefragmentedorchestra.com. 15.8.11

Goda, Y. and Davis, G.W. (2003), 'Mechanisms of synapse assembly and disassembly', *Neuron*, 40, pp. 243–264.

Grant, J., Matthias, J., Hodgson, T. and Miranda E.M. (2009), 'Hearing Thinking', lecture notes in *Computer Science*, Vol. 5484. Proceedings of the EvoWorkshops, 2009 on 'Applications of Evolutionary Computing: EvoMUSART', Berlin, Heidelberg: Springer-Verlag.

Grant, J. (2010), 'Noise: networks, sensation, experience', *The 11th Consciousness Reframed International Research Conference*, Trondheim: Norway.

Hopfield, J.J. and Brody, C.C. (2001), 'What is a Moment? Transient Synchrony as a Collective Mechanism for Spatiotemporal Integration', *Proceeding of National Academy of Science of the United States of America*, 98, 3, pp. 1282–1287.

Ikegaya, Y., Aaron, G., Cossart, R., Aronov, D., Lampl, L., Ferster, D. and Yuste, R. (2004), 'Synfire Chains and cortical songs: Temporal Modules of Cortical Activity', *Science*, 304, pp. 559–564.

Izhikevich, E.M., Gally, J.A. and Edelman, G.M. (2004), 'Spike-Timing Dynamics of Neuronal Groups', *Cerebral Cortex*, 14, pp. 933–944.

Jones, D., Hodgson, T., Grant, J. Matthias, J., Outram, N. and Ryan, N. (2009), 'The Fragmented Orchestra', *Proceedings of New Interfaces for Musical Expression (NIME 2009), Conference*, Carnegie Mellon University, Pittsburgh, PA.), USA, http://nime2009.org/proceedings.php. 15.8.11

Roads, C. (2004), *Microsound*, Cambridge: MIT Press.

Stockhausen, K., (1959), '… how time passes …' [trans. Cornelius Cardew], *Die Reihe*, 3, pp.10–40.

Wood, D.C. (2000), 'Time-shelters: an essay in the poetics of time', in *Time and the Instant*, Robin Durie and David Webb (eds), Manchester: Clinamen Press.

Chapter 5

Ergin Çavuşoğlu and the Art of Betweenness

Tim Cresswell

Introduction

Young men in hoodies play with a street lamp in an anonymous city street. Ships navigate the Bosphorus strait in Istanbul, dark hulks against the lights of the city at night. A man and a woman travel between Turkey and England through little considered low-cost airports. A ship heads towards its fate in a storm off the coast of France. A shore is fogbound as we hear the sound of the sea against land. These are the strange spaces of the video and installation art of Ergin Çavuşoğlu – an artist born as an ethnic Turk in Bulgaria who now lives and practices in London.

This is an in-between world: a world where mobility meets place, where abstraction meets life as it is lived. Borders, points between states, unnoticed remnant spaces of cities; the ocean – these are spaces of liminality, momentarily outside of the norms of place and community and are places in between; places where normal rules are suspended. Some describe them as non-places when in fact they are simply places with a different order (Augé 1995). They are often places associated with travel and transit. Not the kinds of places that have viewpoints and appear in guidebooks but the kinds of place we have to traverse to get from here to there. To some people, refugees and global business people for instance, these are spaces they become stuck in – limbo is a good model for a liminal place. They are sites where we are not encouraged to linger.

The idea of liminality was developed by Victor Turner in *The Ritual Process* and is based on the ideas of Arnold van Gennep (Gennep et al. 1977; Turner 1977). Liminality refers most directly to anthropological observation of rituals that involve a distancing from 'normal' society; a period of transformation (a liminal phase – rites of passage) and a return to some kind of established order. Associated with the liminal phase of a ritual is a form of togetherness not based on formal social hierarchy, referred to as 'communitas'. Applying ideas of liminality to space suggests that there are kinds of space and place that are inhabited by people between states, undergoing rites of passage. An example may be a border separating one set of expected norms from another. Borderlands are often thought of as spaces of mixing where social and cultural rules are suspended and mixed up in a way that produces new kinds of hybrid community (Anzaldua 1987). Liminality also suggests some kind of journey – a leaving of one space and all its expected codes and rules and arrival in another. The journey becomes a period of liminality with its own transitory forms of communitas. We can think of the spaces of a journey – the road, the airport, the train – as liminal spaces.

A liminal place is a zone that often combines the seemingly antithetical worlds of place and mobility, of roots and routes. A model that is often used for place is home – a site where we feel attachment and belonging (Blunt and Dowling 2006) – a site that holds profound meaning in dense and familiar topography. Our lives and worlds are made up of such places – a geography of living out lives, falling in love, being a child, raising children, going to school, working, pursuing the things we enjoy. To tell the story of our lives is often to tell a geography of places. Mobility, on the other hand, is often seen as a means to get between places – dead time, a waste of effort, inefficient (Urry 2007). Despite the grand traditions of stories of voyage from the *Odyssey* onwards, the journey is so often to simply rediscover home, to become reacquainted with place: when Ulysses returns to Ithaca, it is to discover home. Or, as T. S Eliot put it, at the end of *Little Gidding*:

We shall not cease from exploration
And the end of all our exploring
Will be to arrive where we started
And know the place for the first time.

(Eliot 2001: 43)

Mobility is more often seen as a threat to place, as an undoing and as a lack of attachment and commitment – footloose, drifting and purposeless (Cresswell 2006) .

Ergin Çavuşoğlu uses liminal places to examine the intersection of place and the journey in the modern world. Airspaces, seaspace and borderspace, as well as the non-descript spaces of the city are his settings. In so doing, he allows us to consider the intersection of place and the journey. To think about what place might be in the life we lead now in a mobile world. The remainder of this chapter focuses on the different but linked representations of liminal space in a series of Çavuşoğlu's artworks. Let us start with the nightscape of the suburban street.

It is a darkly lit street in a city somewhere. It looks like London but nowhere in particular. We are looking down on the street, apparently from a window, perhaps of a bedroom or an upper story flat. This is the space of the city at night. Not the space of bright lights associated with central city landscapes but the space of the inner suburbs, a space without people. It is a space which is supposed to be empty at night. The setting is utterly banal and unremarkable. There seems to be no reason for it to be the object of a work of art; it is vaguely threatening. It is this setting that forms the backdrop for the strange dances of anonymous adolescents who suspend a mountain bike high up on a sign post or dance around a parked car seemingly oblivious to their role in a short video. We can imagine that such events take place regularly as young men and women (but mostly men) make their way through the after-hours urban nightscape. Despite this assumption these acts are made to seem otherworldly and surreal: the angle of the camera suggests surveillance;

Figure 1. Ergin Çavuşoğlu, *Mountain Bike*, 2003, single channel video,
running time: 2.15 minutes. Soundtrack: 'Sedyankata e ne Razvala'
Bulgarian Folk Ensemble, Philip Koutev composed by Georgi Genov.

it could be a CCTV camera catching its prey at play whilst it turns us into voyeurs of
night life. What we are seeing appears to be the activities of the excluded, in a space time
that is unregulated. Despite the street dances occurring in public space we can assume
the dancers do not think of themselves as being watched. It is as if we are intruding on
something private. These early pieces of video art by Çavuşoğlu seem to reverse a familiar
trope of voyeuristic city life: that of the view into private space from the outside such as

silhouetted bodies behind curtains or peeks into the lives of others from trains passing the backs of houses, as in, for example, the images of Edward Hopper. Here, it seems as if something private is happening in public.

This is the world where we might walk with a slight uneasiness, with no-one else around, anonymous and dark. It is the landscape where the rats emerge, foxes scavenge and teenagers make trouble. Night cultures make temporary liminal spaces of streets that are banal during day-light hours. Night is a particular kind of liminal time long associated with dissent. The image of young people attaching a bike to a signpost reminds me of the Parisian rebels who used to smash gas lanterns at night in a protest against the new surveillent state (Palmer 2000, Schivelbusch 1988).

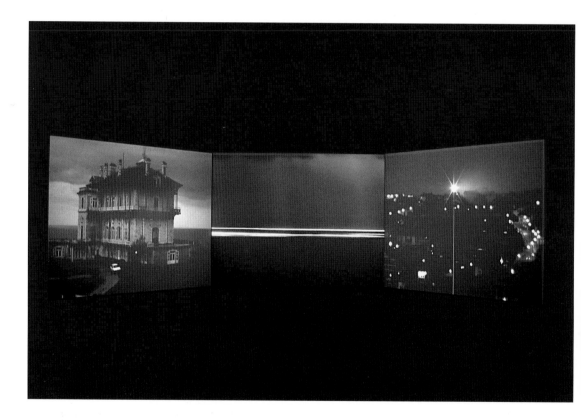

Figure 2. Ergin Çavuşoğlu, *Poised in the Infinite Ocean* (2004), 3-screen video installation, sound (reading from the book 'The Outlaw Sea' by William Langewiesche), 5.20 minutes. Installation view, Manchester Art Gallery, 2006.

Night descends over the south-west coast of France, near Biarritz and an old, un-seaworthy cargo ship making its way north to the bay and getting caught in a storm. A lighthouse flashes; the sea becomes wilder as a storm is on the way, which we watch unfold on three large video screens. A grand but battered chateau stands against the storm as the city around it retreats inside and shuts its doors against the crescendo of elements. We hear a narration about a ship out of the Bay of Biscay confronting the fact of the storm; the ship, we discover, is sailing towards its fate where it will sink. We hear of the ship slowly falling apart.

Although the narrated ship sounds fragile and doomed the chateau seems solid and homely. There may be a family inside playing parlour games around a snug fire; perhaps candles have been lit. Perhaps, on the other hand, this is the home of an elderly woman whose family have all left home. Maybe this place is too big for a solitary inhabitant. Regardless, in the context of a storm and the wild sea, this house asserts itself as place – as a site of attachment and stability in the fluid world around it. The city too seems well protected against the storm. The lighthouse is a fixed point in space; its metronomic signal tells the sailors and ships to stay away. This is a dangerous point for them – there are rocks just under the turbulence of the water. Against these fixities, we know the ship is moving; it has moved from the south and contains stories in its cargo that transcend space. Yet, the ship is also a place. Places are supposed to be richer, more profound, versions of locations (Cresswell 2004; Relph 1976; Tuan 1977), but having a location does not mean being still. A ship has a location and now a GPS system would be able to tell us where it was. This moving location is also a moving place as particular forms of sociality mark ship life. Levi-Strauss (1963) told us this on his journey to Latin America and Malinowski (2002) noted the boat born placeness of the Melanesian sea farers. Foucault (1965) described the 'ship of fools' as a special place – a heterotopia or place outside of place that is both sealed from the world and yet part of the 'infinity of the sea,' that of the infinite ocean. As the narrator reminds us, the ship 'is something of a fantasy, floating free of the realities at sea' (Langewiesche 2006). In recent years, we have seen ships act in heterotopic ways that suggest a different set of orderings. They have become places for the extraordinary and the fantastic and outside of the normal territorial definitions of what belongs and what does not belong. While these ships are suggestive of different forms of order they simultaneously confirm more familiar land-based orderings. Garbage ships, for instance, have crossed the world full of the debris of civilization, looking to unload their toxic cargos in the marginalized places of the developing world. Such ships are formally illegitimate, illegal even, but functionally they make serve to reinforce the ways the globe is ordered. Similarly, ships full of refugees have sailed the Mediterranean and the Pacific looking for a way in to more secure worlds. Ships have anchored at sea, just beyond the jurisdictions of nation states offering tax-free cigarettes and abortions. Ships can be marginal places but they are also the instruments of normality – the lifeblood of the modern world system. They carry the stuff we consume and carry oil to keep us moving. Ships of navies still patrol the seas demanding conformity, policing borders and imposing the will of the mighty on others.

Ships and the sea then are fluid places (Langewiesche 2006; Peters 2010; Steinberg 2001): they do not conform to the hard certainties of land. They are both beyond place and places in and of themselves; spaces where we are able to project our fantasies of freedom; a romantic pirate world of permanent transgression. Yet, they are also the places of slavery, of trade, of the regulation of the world and the imposition of order.

Figure 3. *Downward Straits* (2004) Ergin Çavuşoğlu, *Downward Straits* (2004), video installation, 3 minutes. Installation view, ICA, London.

The sense of the sea as an outlaw space is necessary to construct its 'other' of home as firm and bounded where rootedness forms a site of attachment (Blunt and Dowling 2006). In *Poised in the Infinite Ocean*, Çavuşoğlu works with this world of presence and absence. The home of the chateau and the home of the city seem snug and enclosed as spaces of stable identity and familiarity. They do so because of the wildness of the sea and the storm. Similarly, the unfolding story of the other place – the heterotopic ship would seem less otherworldly if it were not for the reassuring stabilities of landlocked homes. At the same time, the places we see in Çavuşoğlu's work – the homes of the city and the chateau also become ship-like. The story of the ship is told as we see homes bound tight against the weather. These homes will not sink but the threat is there. We never see the ship out in the Bay of Biscay but we know it is there through the narrative we hear. We see the storm, the chateau, the town and the lighthouse. Despite its absence in the video, the presence of buildings against the backdrop of the storm allows us to imagine being bound in the ship, hemmed in by the Infinite Ocean. On the other hand, the chateau seems singular and specific, occupying a point in an infinite world that is stretched forever in all directions. And the home (whether the ship home or the house home) gets its power through its contrast with the unknowability of infinity – the void of nothingness.

Ships move, ghostlike, between two shores; some carry oil whereas some carry containers full of the things we consume. The two shores are often cast as the shores of Europe and Asia. They are the shores of the Bosphorus Strait in Istanbul; it is night time. We can see lights across the waterway. Some of the shots are from one shore and some from the other. The ships move both ways, right to left and left to right, their dark hulls and superstructures move across the lights of the other continent, momentarily blacking them out. Their presence is marked by the absence of light. All of this is happening on four large screens that the viewer is invited to walk through and engage with. The viewer is mobile like the ships, looking right and left as we negotiate our own passage. We hear sound too – the sounds of radio transmissions concerning the regulation of maritime mobilities.

Sector Türkeli, sector Türkeli. Kumamar, *Kunamar.*
Kunamar, sector Türkeli.

We are twenty miles to the pilot station. Our ETA is 1300. Over.
Standby *Kunamar,* standby.
South of the Princess Islands, south of the Princess Islands.
Kunamar, Kumanar, sector Türkelu

Sector Türkeli, this is *Kunamar* come in.
What is your call sign, call sign please?
Time Three, Echo, Alpha, Good, Nine, Over.

(Çavuşoğlu 2006, npn)

As well as being water-borne, the ship is travelling through abstract space – a space of locations and estimated times of arrivals. This is a sphere of codified information that allows things to move with little regard to the histories and particularities of the places that surround them. Ships are the vehicles that make the world work. They seem unremarkable: invisible even. Ships are old. Almost as old as humanity. They move across the earth's surface relatively slowly. They do not attract the attention of the theorists in the way airports or automobiles do. But the vast majority of the world's 'stuff' moves on ships.

Ships are part of the infrastructure of mobility that hides what it is that is moving. Shipping containers are piled high on thousands of ships as they cross the world, they accumulate, however briefly, in massive container ports; then move on trains and trucks from port to warehouse and from warehouse to shops. The vast majority of things that travel the world do so on ships yet they remain remarkably invisible: when we see shipping containers we have no idea what is inside them. The particular mobilities of the container and the ships that carry them rely on their blankness and invisibility, enabling the smooth operation of capitalism, and are at the centre of our everyday lives without us even noticing. But there is another side: any number of TV police dramas uses the container as a site of unwanted ingress, of disease, of weapons or of people labelled 'illegal'. Their blankness is both the source of their efficiency and a source of threat and doubt. There are 300 million containers currently circulating the world whose apparent innocuousness is a deliberate consequence of the modern logistical imperative to standardize movements and to abolish stillness as much as possible. It is this linking of visibility, standardization and routinization that global commodity movements are predicated on. This linking attempts to produce stability and predictability, and in turn invisibility. It also produces the other container – the container that can carry illegal garbage, drugs, arms or smuggled humans invisibly across borders.

Some of the ships that pass through the Bosphorus are tankers. The movement of oil is as mysterious as the movement of things – the lubricant and power source of capitalism. The Bosphorus Strait is a chokepoint for the global supply of oil from the Caspian region to the world; it is narrow and hard to navigate for the leviathan tankers that pass through it at the rate of 5500 annually. Russia is currently building mammoth pipelines across Europe to by-pass this chokepoint. So this space in between is both central and liminal. Central to the infrastructure of a carbon-based economy yet in between –East and West, Europe and Asia, the Caspian and the Mediterranean.

Downward Straits reflects on this largely invisible, mundane, passage of oil and things across the seemingly contourless, borderless waters of the world. These ships only become visible as a kind of absence: the ship-shaped blankness that we perceive as the dim silhouettes of ships pass across the lights of the thoroughly coded landscapes of Europe and Asia. Here, the thin passage of water acts as a liminal zone where mobility is juxtaposed with the seeming certainties of the hard, borderline landscapes that form the shores. The ship is a place outside of place. As in much of Çavuşoğlu's work, a mysterious entanglement of place and mobility occurs asking us to confront the ways in which they make and undo each other.

78

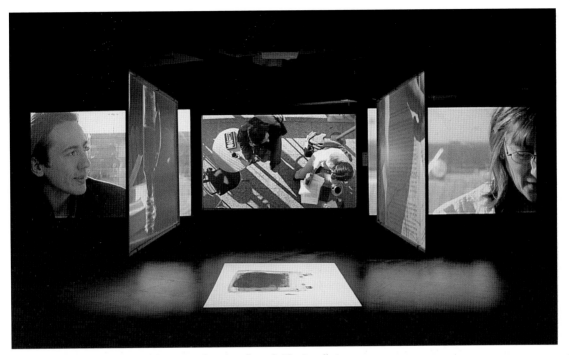

Figure 4. Ergin Çavuşoğlu, *Point of Departure* (2006), 6-channel video installation, three channel sound; 31.36 minutes. Installation view, NGCA Sunderland.

Once again, we are between East and West. This time in transit: in airports, in Stansted in north-east London and Trabzon in Turkey. Trabzon airport is located 7 km from the city, long associated with long distance trade as the Silk Road and an important commercial centre for a series of empires. The airport 'buzzes with local colour and variety' and its 'rhythms are more of the market than the airport terminus' (Çavuşoğlu 2006). Stansted airport, a modernist classic designed by Norman Foster, services the growing low-cost flight industry: it is 'efficient and polite;' designed to deal with 'at-risk' flights approaching London with facilities to keep planes away from the media, the terminal and passengers (Çavuşoğlu 2006). Both places were sites of Roman roads and can be conceived of as, in the artist's terms 'the end points of the European Idea' (Çavuşoğlu 2006).

We see these airports on five large video screens that we inhabit when we walk between them. On the floor in the centre of the piece, the viewer sees a projection of luggage passing through an X-ray machine. She sees the view from security of, as it were, the insides of people's lives. The bags follow a rhythmic to and fro, and provide an underlying pulse to the story that unfolds. Just as the bags are surveilled and handled so are the passengers who pass through where people, like bags, are processed. As we become familiar with the piece we follow the travels of two characters and the different ways they inhabit the airports – one, a man who is a Turkish academic travelling from Trabzon to Stansted and the other, a female English journalist travelling from Stansted to Damscus, Baghdad and Eastern Anatolia (Turkey) before returning to Stansted. The cool efficiency of Stansted contrasts with the airport at Trabzon where the academic can sit and smoke a cigarette. We see our passengers pass through security checks and the differences that implies for a man travelling from east to west, and white woman travelling in the opposite direction.

Airports have been described as the non-place *par excellence* (Augé 1995). They are sites associated with transit where we give ourselves over to the need to follow signs and commands. They are liminal as the traveller is between places and only there in order to make a connection. A strange kind of sociality exists between people who only share the need to get somewhere where we follow directions and are processed. Some have seen a special kind of freedom and utopian redemption in airport space (Ballard 1997; Braidotti 1994; Chambers 1994); others see travail and rigid class and national distinctions (Crang 2002; Cresswell 2006). Çavuşoğlu's (2006) *Point of Departure* encourages us to think of the airport as a space of difference, showing different airports with different embedded histories and the kinds of connections that exist between the 'end points of the European Idea'. The airports themselves are very different as they are the kinds of travels that might link them.

In Çavuşoğlu's installation, the sense of rhythmic processing is powerful and pervasive and structures the space of the viewer. The complicated arrangement of screens along with the projection on the floor allows the viewer to move around, as if a passenger. The sound is engineered so that you move between different soundscapes always hearing the hum and rhythm of the bags and people being processed, creating a sense of life being abstracted – the lack of 'authenticity' associated with non-places. But at the same time, the viewer experiences the highly personal and different trajectories of the two travellers that undercut the sense of the abstract. The liminal space of the airport combines a sense of abstraction and lives being lived and identities formed along routes.

Conclusions

A question for artists in the twenty-first century and for Çavuşoğlu in particular, is how to record a world torn between place and motion. On the one hand, there is the possibility of using art to contest a mobile world – to insist on the value and authenticity of place and to establish roots. On the other hand, there is the possibility of denying place, of celebrating a world in motion where nothing stays anywhere for very long. The magic of Çavuşoğlu's work is its refusal to embrace either of these easy extremes. Instead, much of his work meditates on the inter-relations of place and mobility and in the spaces of liminality – places were identity hangs in the balance. His is a traveller's world of borderlands and in-between spaces. Çavuşoğlu appears to be perpetually caught in a world on the move, in the city, on the sea, in airports, in the places of the migrant. Spaces such as these are key spaces in the modern world. The world has always been one of both roots and routes, but now this tension is becoming ever more evident. Issues of migration may be among the most important of our age, and governments act in reactionary ways to make the place of the nation more like a fortress. Meanwhile, the outsiders: the strangers and foreigners are 'stuck' in an 'infinite ocean' of movement, on the margins. Their places are precarious and include the margins of the cities – under highways or on leaky unseaworthy vessels crossing turbulent oceans. At the same time, a kinetic elite inhabits a carefully regulated space of flows – the airport lounge, the business centre and the first-class cabin. As a Turk, brought up in Bulgaria and living in London, Çavuşoğlu imaginatively inhabits in-between spaces. Spaces that are both part of the way the world is structured and laden with the possibility of its undoing. His video installations combine to form an art of precarious places in a mobile and sometimes threatening world.

References

Anzaldua, Gloria (1987), *Borderlands: La frontera*, San Francisco: Aunt Lute Books.

Augé, Marc (1995), *Non-Places: Introduction to an Anthropology of Supermodernity*, London and New York: Verso.

Ballard, J.G. (1997), 'Going Somewhere?' *The Observer*, London, p. 11.

Blunt, Alison and Dowling, Robyn (2006), *Home (Key Ideas in Geography)*, London: Routledge.

Braidotti, Rosi (1994), *Nomadic Subjects: Embodiment and Sexual Difference in Contemporary Feminist Theory*, New York: Columbia University Press.

Çavuşoğlu, Ergin (2006), *Places of Departure*, Film and Video Umbrella, London.

Chambers, Iain (1994), *Migrancy, Culture, Identity*, Routledge: London.

Crang, Mike (2002), 'Between Places: Producing Hubs, Flows, and Networks' *Environment and Planning A*, 34, pp. 569–574.

Cresswell, Tim (2004), *Place: A Short Introduction*, Oxford: Blackwell.

Cresswell, Tim (2006), *On the Move: Mobility in the Modern Western World*, New York: Routledge.

Eliot, T.S. (2001), *Four Quartets*, London: Faber & Faber.

Foucault, Michel (1965), *Madness and Civilization : A History of Insanity in the Age of Reason*, New York: Vintage.

Goetz, I. and Urbaschek, S. (eds) (2010), *Fast Forward 2: The Power of Motion*, Ostfildern: Hatje Cantz.

Langewiesche, William (2006), *The Outlaw Sea: Chaos and Crime on the World's Oceans*, London: Granta.

Levi-Strauss, Claude (1963), *Tristes Tropiques: Anthropological Study of Primitive Societies in Brazil*, New York: Atheneum.

Malinowski, Bronislov (2002), *Argonauts of the Western Pacific: An Account of Native Enterprise and Adventure in the Archipelagoes of Melanesian New Guinea*, London: Routledge.

Palmer, Bryan D. (2000), *Cultures of Darkness: Night Travels in the Histories of Transgression*, New York: Monthly Review Press.

Peters, Keith (2010), 'Future Promises for Contemporary Social and Cultural Geographies of the Sea', *Geography Compass*, 4, pp. 1260–1272.

Relph, E. and Scott, Allen J. (2008), *Place and Placelessness*, London: Pion.

Schivelbusch, Wolfgang (1988), *Disenchanted Night: The Industrialisation of Light in the Nineteenth Century*, New York: Berg Publishers.

Steinberg, Philip E. (2001), *The Social Construction of the Ocean*, Cambridge: Cambridge University Press.

Tuan, Yi-Fu (2001), *Space and Place: The Perspective of Experience*, Minneapolis: University of Minnesota Press.

Turner, Victor Witter (1995), *The Ritual Process: Structure and Anti-Structure (Foundations of Human Behaviour)*, Ithaca, NY: Cornell University Press.

Urry, John (2007), *Mobilities*, Cambridge: Polity.

Van Gennep, Arnold (1961) *The Rites of Passage*, London: Routledge and Kegan Paul.

Notes

The chapter is an extension of ideas developed from catalogue entries in Goetz, I. and Urbaschek, S. (eds), (2010) *Fast Forward 2. The Power of Motion*, Hatje Cantz: Ostfildern.

Chapter 6

Daniel Buren's Theoretical Practice

Dominic Rahtz

The art of the 1960s can be defined by two main tendencies, namely, impersonality and literalism. The first involved an absence of self, or the negation of signs of self: in the work of art, a tendency that can be associated first of all with such artists as Frank Stella or Andy Warhol, which then developed into what appears as a precipitous succession of movements – Earthworks, Conceptual Art, Process Art and so on – that sought to define the work of art in the impersonal terms of materiality or language. Literalism can be seen as the other side of the same development, developing from a concern with the object or thing-like character of the work of art, to considerations of the situation of this object within a wider reality, seen in phenomenological or institutional terms. These two tendencies may be seen in retrospect to be symptomatic of a changed relationship between art and reality. During the late 1960s and into the early 1970s, there were repeated attempts to bring the real world into the domain of art. One thinks, for example, of a work such as Hans Haacke's censored *Shapolsky et al. Manhattan Real-Estate Holdings: A Real-Time Social System, as of May 1, 1971* (1971), a work that adopted the political mode of information as *exposé* concerning a particular social and economic reality. Conversely, there were attempts to take art into the domain of reality, as in the *Affichages sauvages* of the French artist Daniel Buren, in which his work in the form of posters were pasted up in spaces usually reserved for advertising in the streets of Paris and other cities.

In the case of Buren, this relationship between art and reality can almost be regarded as constitutive of his work in general. In an essay first published in 1981, the art historian and critic Benjamin Buchloh (2000: 126) characterized the condition of Buren's work in terms of its 'permanent shift between being an aesthetic sign and an element of everyday perceptual reality'. According to Buchloh, this 'permanent shift' between art and reality prevented Buren's work from collapsing into either the totalizing ideological determinations of the society of the spectacle on one side or the irrelevance of art with respect to this social reality on the other. It is possible, however, that Buren's work is not an oscillation between two conditions, but rather consists in a separate position that Buren maintained with respect to both art and reality. It is noticeable, for example, that in his texts Buren often characterized his work as a form of 'theory'. And one wonders what the art critic Michel Claura meant when he stated of Buren in 1969 that 'Clearly it is no longer an artist who is speaking, but a theoretician. Theory and art are incompatible' (Claura 1969: 48). If 'theory' designates a shift in intellectual history where the issue of the relationship between a mode of representation, such as art, and the reality it represents produced its own separate discourse, then Buren's identification of his work with theory may be said to provide it with a position from which to reflect or act on the relationship between art and reality, without necessarily being one or the other.

In texts published in the late 1960s and 1970s, Buren reversed the usual distinction made between practice and theory, claiming that the texts he wrote were not theoretical and that theory was only produced in the practice of his work. In the preface to his 1973 collection *Five Texts*, Buren explained that the function of his texts was rather to recognize the relationships – ideological, aesthetic, and so on – that determined the domain of art in which his work was situated (Buren 1973: 7–8). For him, this recognition was not in itself theoretical, but rather revealed the realm in which the practice of his work, as theory, which always preceded the texts, was produced. The text in which Buren defined

Figure 1. Daniel Buren, Photo-souvenir: *Affichage sauvage*, April 1968, work *in situ*, Paris (photo: Bernard Boyer). Copyright: ADAGP, Paris and DACS, London 2011.

this particular meaning of theory was entitled 'Beware!', first published in 1969 in French with the title 'Mise en garde' in the catalogue for the exhibition of Conceptual Art, 'Conception,' at the Städtischen Museum in Leverkusen, Germany, and then revised and translated for subsequent publications, including the British art journal *Studio International* in 1970. Although the text begins with an attempt to distance his work from the contemporary conceptual art to which his work was often related, 'Beware!' was principally concerned with a description of the formal characteristics of Buren's own work and with its epistemological and political consequences as theory.

In the second section of 'Beware!', Buren described his work in terms of a conception of form that was negated internally through sameness and externally through difference. This conception of form was referred throughout the text as a 'zero degree' or 'neutral degree of form,' a reference to Roland Barthes' 1953 book *Writing Degree Zero*, which developed a view of modern literary form as concerned with its own specificity as literary language, defined by its negation of the conventions of literary style and representation. In Buren's work, a similar kind of formal neutrality was achieved through a series of determinate negations of conventional artistic form, concentrated mainly on the elimination of difference within what would normally be regarded as the interiority of the pictorial field, but also with regard to works of art as forms of representation (which he regarded variously as 'hallucinations' or 'illusions'). This negation of artistic form depended on the sameness of the pattern of stripes, which remained the same whether the stripes were those of the canvas awning material Buren appropriated or printed on paper. The stripes were always of the same width, more or less 8.7 cm, and the interior relationship between the stripes was that of mere alternation and repetition. Although Buren allowed for changes in colour, only one colour, which could be any colour, was used within any particular work, alternating with white (Buren 1970a: 101, 102).

The repetition of this pattern from work to work prevented any formal relationship being established between the stripes that constituted the surface of the work (what Buren later referred to as its 'material' or as a 'tool') and the varying literal shape of this surface, so that surface and literal shape appeared to have nothing to do with each other, defined in their relation by mutual indifference. The repetition from work to work also produced the sense of a lack of development that was opposed to the formal development he associated with modern art (Buren 1970a: 101, 102). In this sense, the repetition of the work gave it a position of exteriority with respect to the history of modern art and hence a more properly historical existence, the work thus passing from the 'mythical' to the 'historical,' in the sense of Barthes' distinction between these terms in the theoretical section of his book *Mythologies*. The different realizations of the work, whether it was realized in an interior or exterior space, whether hung as canvas or pasted up as paper, were also repetitions of the negation of form in the work. The repetition occurred as an 'effacement' or a 'cancelling-out' of the form of the work, or, more particularly, of such conventional artistic values as style and originality. As these values were also inseparable from the self of the artist, their 'effacement' also entailed the negation of artistic self.

The beginnings of Buren's practice are usually located in the series of performances he staged with Olivier Mosset, Michel Parmentier and Niele Toroni during 1967 in Paris and elsewhere, which drew attention to the situations in which the paintings were produced and shown. As part of the group's first *Manifestation*, at the Salon de la Jeune Peinture, Musée d'Art Moderne de la Ville de Paris on 3 January 1967, each artist produced paintings *in situ* with standardized motifs. Buren's motif was derived from a light grey and white striped canvas awning, already fabricated as a commercially available material. This material was mounted on stretchers of about two metres square, with the outermost grey stripes painted over with white acrylic paint. Later the same day, the four artists took down their paintings, replacing them with a banner that declared 'Buren, Mosset, Parmentier, Toroni, do not exhibit' (Buchloh 2008: 311; Lippard 1997: 24).

Part of the rhetoric that surrounded the actions of 1967 was concerned with the impersonality of the motifs and their mode of production. This was demonstrated in an exhibition held at Paris in December 1967 in which Buren, Mosset and Toroni each painted the motifs of the others in addition to their own, and again in an exhibition the same month at Lugano in Switzerland, in which Buren and Mosset invited visitors to complete their paintings. In an interview with André Parinaud in *Galerie des Arts* in February 1968, Buren stated 'My painting, at the limit, can only signify itself. *It is*. So much so, and so well, that anybody can make it and claim it. It is outside of me...' (Lippard 1997: 43). In a text accompanying these exhibitions and in very similar language, Michel Claura wrote that there was 'an *absolute* identity among all the canvases of each "type," whoever happened to be the author of any one of them. [...] For the first time, with Buren, Mosset, Toroni, painting *is*' (Claura, in Alberro and Stimson 1999: 30). In the section of 'Beware!' that dealt with 'anonymity', impersonality was defined in terms of the negation of artistic self in the work, as opposed to what might be called the empirical self of the artist that existed outside the work. Impersonality tended to be defined in terms that related his work to contemporary literary theory, as if Buren was concerned to isolate, in the realm of art, the 'literariness' that constituted the theoretical object of critics such as Barthes or Maurice Blanchot.

The definition of impersonality was raised again in a text written later in 1969, titled 'It Rains, It Snows, It Paints,' first published in English in *Arts Magazine* in 1970. This essay began by describing the futility of contemporary trends in which art was continually being negated by its opposite, by forms of 'anti-art,' resulting in a loss of meaning and the possible disappearance of art. Buren went on to suggest, with reference to a passage from Blanchot's *The Space of Literature*, that this condition also revealed the essential mode of existence of the work of art.

> Why then, even as it is about to disappear, when its existence has lost all justification, '*does art appear* for the first time to constitute a search for something essential; what counts is no longer the artist, or his feelings, or holding up a mirror to mankind, or man's labor, or any of the values on which our world is built, or those other values of

which the world beyond once held a promise. Yet art is nevertheless an inquiry, precise and rigorous, that can be carried out only within a work, *a work of which nothing can be said, except that it is.*'

(Buren 1970b: 42)

This definition of the work of art required an impersonality that allowed the work to question its own mode of being in a way that was analogous to Blanchot's definition of the specificity of the literary work.

In *The Space of Literature*, the mode of existence of the work of art was defined by its separateness, not only from the world, but also from the author. According to Blanchot, the literary work only stated its own existence and thereby established its own specifically literary space. Although the medium of the literary work was language, in the space of literature language was not considered in terms of a representation of the world, but rather as a representation of itself. For Blanchot, the writer necessarily began with literary language, rather than the world, which meant that the literary work was not to be seen as *after* the world in the same way that a representation might be considered *after* what it represents. Literary language preserved the negativity that separated language from the world.

'To write', Blanchot wrote, 'is to withdraw language from the world …', from the world of 'action and time' (Blanchot 1982: 26). As the self of the writer was defined according to this world of action and time, the literary work, in its separateness from the world, necessarily excluded this self. The radical character of the impersonal interiority of the literary work can be read in Blanchot's interpretation of certain statements by Mallarmé, in which the difference between the writer and the work was that of an incommensurability between different modes of existence, one involving the self and one involving its absence. The self of the reader was similarly excluded from the literary work to the extent that their reading corresponded to the separate and specifically literary existence of the work. In his 1966 essay on Blanchot, the literary theorist Paul de Man described the movement in Blanchot's criticism whereby '[b]oth [author and reader] move beyond their respective particularity toward a common ground that contains both of them, united by the impulse that makes them turn away from their particular selves' (de Man 1989: 64). This 'common ground' of the work constituted the space of literature, its separate and impersonal mode of existence.

The withdrawal of the literary work from the realm of action raised the question of the relationship between the work and the action of the artist. This question would take on a particular importance in the years around 1968, because it was a period that can be characterized on one hand by an impulse to act politically and collectively on the part of artists, and on the other by artistic tendencies that sought to negate the separation of art from the world of action. In characterizing the critical position of Blanchot, it is significant that it was partly developed out of a critique of Jean-Paul Sartre's argument for an engaged literature defined as an action in the world like other actions, and therefore part of history. For Blanchot, the literary work was not an action defined in historical terms, and neither could it be seen as a product of labour in terms of labour in general. In a chapter in *The Space of Literature* entitled 'The Future and the Question of Art', Blanchot considered the position of art within a general history of the realization of the world, seen in Hegelian terms. Within this perspective, art could be turned outwards and realized in the world, and in so doing contribute to its general history (although in reality it could only be a poor substitute for historically significant or political actions). Or art could be turned inwards, concerned with its own workings, but nevertheless contributing to the realization of the world because of the exemplary character of artistic action for action in general (Blanchot 1982: 211–219). For Blanchot, the difficulty with these two possible definitions of art was that they remained centred on the action of the artist and not on the work itself. To these definitions, he opposed the condition of the work as the realization of its own specific mode of existence, which was opposed to, or in excess of, the historical realization of the world. At the end of the section concerned, Blanchot considered the question of why the realm of history and action, of 'the artist or active labour', appeared to be displaced by a concern with the work itself, 'a work which *is*, and nothing more' (Blanchot 1982: 220). It was this passage that Buren quoted in 'It Rains, It Snows, It Paints.'

The negation of form in Buren's patterns of stripes entailed a particular condition in which the work put into question its own appearance, to the extent that form can be regarded as the conventional condition of appearance of works of art. In effect, the work stated its own existence in the form of a question regarding its own possibility – 'the object questioning its own disappearance as object' in Buren's enigmatic and circular phrase (Buren 1970b: 43). The separate and impersonal mode of existence of the work, furthermore, entailed certain kinds of relationship between art and action. As the impersonality of the work of art necessarily excluded the self of the artist, it also excluded the possibility of any action on the part of this self.

Yet, it would be a distortion to suggest that the separate and impersonal interiority of the work of art defined in these terms meant that it had no reality in the realm of political action. It is significant, for example, that Herbert Marcuse, an important figure for the New Left in the 1960s, particularly in the United States, referred to Blanchot's idea of 'refusal' in his conclusion to *One-Dimensional Man* (Marcuse 1991: 255–256). Blanchot himself was a participant in the events of May 1968 in Paris, and wrote an unsigned text in 1968 entitled 'Tracts, affiches, bulletin' which dealt with the impersonal modes of writing that were found in the inscriptions or posters on the walls of the streets of Paris that effectively produced a new space of separateness (Hill 1997: 216–217). This space, the 'common ground' produced by a turning away from self, implied a collectivity in political terms. In a similar way, the impersonality and separateness of the work of art, what Blanchot referred to as the space of literature, could be seen as containing a political possibility related to its negative condition with respect to the world.

In the final section of 'Beware!', given the subheading 'Preamble' in the later version of the text, Buren addressed some of the epistemological and political consequences of his work. The text of this section appropriated terms, and at times the style of expression, from the French philosopher Louis Althusser, in particular from the essays published in the early to mid-1960s concerned with a philosophical re-reading of Marx. In the first French version, this final section of 'Beware!' was more revealingly titled 'Théorie – Practique – Rupture' because it was concerned with the relationships between these three terms. The rupture with which Buren was concerned was that of a rupture with art, a prior stage of which consisted in a revision or deconstruction of its history (which for Buren primarily meant in its modernist sense) to establish what he called the 'realities' that defined art. In the first French version of the text, the term 'vérité' (truth) was used instead of the term 'reality', which gave a sense of the epistemological issues at stake (Buren 1969). The provisional nature of these terms, 'truth'/'reality', which was always signalled in the text with quotation marks, was such because in the practice of art they were *recognized* rather than *known*, a distinction Buren derived from Althusser, who had written that 'the (practical) *recognition* of an existence cannot pass for a *knowledge* (i.e. for *theory*)' (Althusser 1969: 166). The rupture that Buren referred to thus lay in the difference between recognizing and knowing, a difference that constituted an 'epistemological break' in Althusser's (1969: 167) terms. In Buren's text, as in Althusser's, the distinction between recognition and knowledge corresponded to that between practice and theory. Buren wrote, 'This recognition of their existence [that is, of "certain problems" signalled in the practice of art] can be called practice. The exact knowledge of these problems will be called theory' (Buren 1970a: 104).

In an important passage at the end of 'Beware!', Buren went on to define 'theory' in the following terms:

We can say, on the basis of the foregoing, that the rupture, if any, can be (can only be) epistemological. This rupture is/will be the resulting logic of a theoretical work at the moment when the history of art (which is still to be made) and its application are/will be envisaged theoretically; theory and theory alone, as we well know, can make possible a revolutionary practice. Furthermore, not only is/will theory be indissociable from its own practice, but again it may/will be able to give rise to other original kinds of practice.

Finally, as far as we are concerned, *it must be clearly understood that when theory is considered as producer/creator, the only theory or theoretic practice is the result presented/the painting* or, according to Althusser's definition: 'Theory: a specific form of practice'.

(Buren 1970a: 104)

Buren thus identified his artistic work with the work of theory. This theory produced a knowledge of the reality of art, as opposed to a recognition, and so represented an epistemological rupture with art. It is clear from the passage that theory also had a political or 'revolutionary' character, in the sense that it provided the epistemological conditions for revolutionary action. The phrase 'theory and theory alone...can make possible a revolutionary practice' in the passage quoted above is itself a reference to Lenin, a reference also made by Althusser in his own justification of theory.

In considering this passage, we have moved from a conception of the mode of existence of the work of art defined according to its impersonality and separation from the world of action to one that consists of a production of knowledge that is also political. In 'Beware!', this political character was articulated subsequent to the mass political movement by workers and students that affected all areas of French society during 1968, including art. Buren was, like Blanchot, a participant in the events of May 1968. During this period, the normal functioning of the art world was temporarily suspended, and, according to some critics, spontaneous and collective political actions effectively replaced the impulse to produce art, and revealed the complicity of the institution of art with the state and with the capitalist economy. These political actions required a mode of artistic production that had the same spontaneity and collectivity, which was realized in the collective and anonymous production at the occupied École des Beaux Arts during May of silk-screened posters used in political protest against President de Gaulle or the Compagnies Républicaines de Sécurité (or riot police). Buren was one of the artists who participated in this production of posters (Buren 1998: 23). His artistic work, however, defined in terms of knowledge and theory, occupied a very different space from the political posters that were immersed in a particular political reality, even as, at particular moments, his work occupied the same literal space.

During 1968, and particularly during April and May of that year, Buren worked with paper printed with green stripes, producing a number of related works realized under the common title of *Proposition didactique* (Lippard 1997: 45). From December 1967, pieces of the striped paper had been posted out anonymously. In the *Affichages sauvages*, pieces of the striped paper were pasted up as posters of varying sizes in more than 200 locations throughout Paris during April, in spaces usually occupied by advertising or notices. Like the posted pieces of paper, this work was anonymous, as well as unauthorized. Then, as part of the '24e Salon de Mai' at the Musée d'Art Moderne de la Ville de Paris, Buren covered a section of the gallery wall, from the ceiling and almost to the floor, with the striped paper, producing a work of approximately 5 metres high and 18 metres long. The gallery work was conventionally identified as the work of the artist, Daniel Buren. Finally, on several occasions, two men walked the streets of Paris carrying panels of the same striped paper in a work called *Hommes-sandwichs* (Fuchs 1976: 4).

The different realizations of the work involved the inside and outside of the museum, the anonymous and the named, the static and the moving, the relationship between the striped surface and the literalness of the support, the relationships in space between the different works, and so on, resulting in a structure of opposing terms. The relationships

Figure 2. Daniel Buren, Photo-souvenir: *Affichage sauvage*,
April 1968, work *in situ*, Paris (photo: Bernard Boyer).
Copyright: ADAGP, Paris and DACS, London 2011.

between the different works prevented them from taking on the condition of art or reality, because the sameness of the pattern of stripes produced a continuity in condition that could not be identified with either. In their lack of determination by the literal shape of the surface or the literalness of the support, the pattern of stripes was indifferent to this literalness. In the streets of Paris, this indifferent condition could take on particular kinds of relationships with its surroundings. The 'zero degree' of form within *Proposition didactique* shifted the concerns of the work to its relationship to what was outside it, giving it, according to Buren, an '*indicative*' or '*critical*' character regarding this exteriority that not only included the situation in which the work was placed, but also the mode of practice that produced the work.

In the case of the *Affichages sauvages*, their immediate surroundings most often consisted of hoardings for advertisements – for products such as washing machines, publicity for films and theatrical performances, and so on, but they were also put up in places such as street corners where there appeared more spontaneous and unauthorized notices or inscriptions. For example, one of Buren's *Photo-souvenirs*, as he termed the photographic documentation of his works, shows a poster of green and white stripes underneath a notice stating 'Yankees-Nazis – hors du Vietnam,' both adjacent to an official notice forbidding notices or posters. Buren's work may be seen to occupy the same places as those impersonal modes of inscription that Blanchot wrote about in the wake of the events of May, but if Buren's work is seen as defined by an impersonality arrived at through the negation of artistic conventions, the relationship between them, in artistic terms, could only be one of discontinuity. In a different register, however, the *Affichages sauvages* could be regarded as instances of action taking place in the real world. Frequently, the posters were put up partially concealing advertisements, and in that sense could be regarded as critical of a consumerist, capitalist society, but in one particularly problematic instance that raised the question of the relationship between art and political action, one of Buren's posters partly obscured a notice put up by an action committee announcing a meeting and describing the conditions at the Nanterre campus of the University of Paris following the revolt of students there. In artistic terms, this instance confirmed the indifference of the pattern of stripes, but in the world of action and history, the partial concealment of the political notice raised the question of the intentionality of the act. The relationship between the intentionality of the act and the impersonality of the work produced a contradiction that is difficult to resolve.

The particular historical moment of May 1968 appeared to reveal an irreconcilability between art and the world of political action. This irreconcilability took on a particular reality when, in May, the exhibition that included the element of *Proposition didactique* consisting of striped paper covering the wall of the gallery was interrupted by the closure of the museum as a consequence of the political actions that occurred at the same time in Paris (Buren 2010). In a sense, this real event produced the same sense of the reality of the ideological complicity of the institution of art with the state that Buren had been seeking to recognize in his texts. However, Buren's own work occupied a different position with regard to this reality. It is clear, returning to the text of 'Beware!', that the theory or knowledge concerned was in Buren's terms, necessarily in a determinate relationship with art, but art defined in terms of the reality of art as an institution. For Buren, following Althusser's definition of 'theoretical practice,' the theory was defined as a practice in relation to the area of practice of which it produced a knowledge. To clarify this definition further, it is necessary to return to the text where it first appeared.

The principal terms of Althusser's definition of theoretical practice can be found in his essay 'On the Materialist Dialectic,' an essay written in 1963 and collected in his 1965 book *For Marx*. Theory, for Althusser, constituted a particular mode of practice, or, more precisely, a 'level' of practice. Practice in its most general sense consisted of the action of forming, according to which a given material was worked on to produce a new form. It is significant that in the original French version of 'Beware!', Buren used the word *'travail'* rather than *'oeuvre'* to refer to his work, which situated it closer to labour as an action of forming than to the traditional work of art or to the literary work as defined by Blanchot. In the practice of theory, the material that was worked consisted of the already existing ideas or representations that constituted a knowledge of the 'reality' to which the theory was oriented. These ideas and representations could be ideologically determined and have the same kind of relationship to 'reality' as more obviously ideological practices such as art. Theory as a practice acted on this material by way of the concepts and methods that had arisen as appropriate to it, within a given area of knowledge. The new form produced through theory was a form of knowledge that differed from the already existing ideas or representations that constituted the material of theory by virtue of its being subject to an action of forming. The extent to which this resulting knowledge corresponded to reality depended on the extent to which it had freed itself from the ideological character of its material. And, according to Althusser, the only way of determining the extent to which knowledge was free from ideology was through the Marxist critique of ideology that effectively provided the theory of theory.

This view of theory entailed a particular kind of relationship between theory and the 'reality' concerned. For Althusser, theory produced a knowledge of reality but this reality only came to be known through the action of theory, by way of its means, acting on its material. In a slightly different context, he wrote:

> ... the real is the real object that exists independently of its knowledge—but which can only be defined by its knowledge. In this second, theoretical, relation, the real is identical with the means of knowing it, the real is its known or to-be-known structure...

(Althusser 1969: 246)

The assumption of a reality prior to and outside of theory to which it was necessarily oriented was, from the point of view of theory, an ideological error. Althusser argued that the relationship between theory and reality was such that the latter was an *effect* rather than a cause, an effect of knowledge produced in the realm of theory. There is thus a sense of circularity in Althusser's conception of the relationship between knowledge and reality, as he acknowledged (Althusser and Balibar 1970: 34). This circle was that described by the relationship between knowledge defined by its relationship to reality and knowledge as something produced. In one of the movements that defined the circle, reality determined the knowledge of it, and in the other the action of producing knowledge, that is, theoretical practice determined the reality that came to be known. Each determined the other.

In considering the two principal references found in Buren's texts of the late 1960s, to Blanchot and Althusser, we are left with two stages of a movement that circumscribes the development of Buren's work during this period. In an initial stage, prior to both methodological terms and in time, Buren produced a negation of artistic self and form in the work of art. This negation was directed at isolating the condition of the work of art from any exteriority. The self of the artist was one such exteriority, usually considered an aspect of the interiority of the modern work of art. In negating this artistic self, Buren produced an impersonality that was defined in artistic terms and, following Blanchot, constituted a particular kind of space, characterized by its separateness. Impersonality can be seen as a preliminary stage in the definition of Buren's work as theoretical practice because it worked negatively against the ideological pre-suppositions that determined the definition of art. From 1968, however, this artistic impersonality or separateness from reality was in a second stage taken into a particular reality – the streets of Paris and other cities – producing the sense of an irreconcilability between two modes of existence. This irreconcilability can be seen as thematized in Buren's work in the mutual indifference between its surface as a pattern of stripes that always stayed the same and the literalness of the shape of the surface or of its support that was always different and part of reality. Buren's work could then refer to an exteriority or reality from the position of the separate and impersonal interiority of the work, which gave it its ‘*indicative*’ or ‘*critical*’ character.

At the end of ‘Beware!’, Buren had asserted that his work was the work of a theoretical practice, defined in terms derived from Althusser. The separate and impersonal interiority of the work would then be the result of an action of forming that took as its material the already existing ideas and representations, which constituted the reality of art. Just as the artistic self was negated to produce an impersonality, the artistic act was negated to allow for the action of theory. It is noticeable that in the final sentence of ‘Beware!’, Buren stated that it was theory, which was the ‘*producer/creator*‘ of the work. Thus, theory did not only represent a particular kind of space, that of the separate and impersonal interiority of the work, but it also represented a particular mode of action. Within the realm of art, this theoretical action produced a knowledge of the reality of art. To the extent that Buren's definition of theoretical practice was faithful to the epistemological circularity of Althusser's definition, the resulting reality of art could only be the production of the theory of art.

References

Alberro, Alexander and Stimson, Blake (eds) (1999), *Conceptual Art: A Critical Anthology*, Cambridge, MA and London: MIT Press.

Althusser, Louis (1969), *For Marx*, trans. Ben Brewster, London: New Left Books.

Althusser, Louis and Balibar, Etienne (1970), *Reading Capital*, trans. Ben Brewster, London: New Left Books.

Blanchot, Maurice (1982), *The Space of Literature*, trans. Ann Smock, Lincoln: University of Nebraska Press.

Buchloh, Benjamin H.D. (2000), 'The Museum and the Monument: Daniel Buren's *Les Couleurs/Les Formes*', in *Neo-Avantgarde and Culture Industry: Essays on European and American Art from 1955 to 1975*, Cambridge, MA and London: MIT Press.

Buchloh, Benjamin H.D. (2008), 'The Group That Was (Not) One: Daniel Buren and BMPT', *Artforum*, 46: 9, pp. 311–313.

Buren, Daniel (1969), 'Mise En Garde' in Rolf Wedewer and Konrad Fischer, *Konzeption – Conception*, Köln and Opladen: Westdeustchen Verlag, n.p.

Buren, Daniel (1970a), 'Beware!', *Studio International*, 179: 920, pp. 100–104.

Buren, Daniel (1970b), 'It Rains, It Snows, It Paints', *Arts Magazine*, 44: 6, p. 43.

Buren, Daniel (1973), 'Preface: Why Write Texts, or The Place from Where I Act', in *Five Texts*, New York and London: John Weber Gallery and Jack Wendler Gallery.

Buren, Daniel (1998), *Au Sujet de...Entretien avec Jérôme Sans*, Paris: Flammarion.

Buren, Daniel (2010), *Catalogue Raisonné, Vol. 3, 1967–1969*, http://catalogue.danielburen.com/fr/. Accessed 11 March 2011.

Claura, Michel (1969), 'Paris Commentary', *Studio International*, 177: 907, pp. 47–49.

de Man, Paul (1989), 'Impersonality in the Criticism of Maurice Blanchot', in *Blindness and Insight: Essays in the Rhetoric of Contemporary Criticism*, London: Routledge.

Fuchs, R.H. (1976), *Discordance/Cohérence*, Eindhoven: Van Abbemuseum.

Hill, Leslie (1997), *Blanchot: Extreme Contemporary*, London and New York: Routledge.

Lippard, Lucy R. (1997), *Six Years: The Dematerialization of the Art Object*, Berkeley, Los Angeles and London: University of California Press.

Marcuse, Herbert (1991), *One-Dimensional Man*, London: Routledge.

Chapter 7

Smuggler-Objects: The Material Culture of Alternative Mobilities

Craig Martin

Introduction

The scene is a familiar one. Queues of people depositing oversized plastic water bottles in specially assigned bins, others hurriedly transferring appropriately sized bottles of toiletries and cosmetics into clear plastic bags. Such security procedures and protocols are part of an extended network of securitization instituted to thwart potential terrorist threat to the stability of global air travel. Following the discovery of the plot to secrete liquid explosives in soft drink bottles onto transatlantic aircraft travelling from the United Kingdom to the United States, it became evident that terrorism utilized ubiquitous items common to global air travel (Laville et al. 2006). The smuggling of these mundane objects onto aircraft demonstrates their taken-for-granted status within consumer culture, appearing almost invisible. Although the consequences of these actions are clearly catastrophic, the role of such common items in terrorist activity reveals how apparently mundane objects hold within them the potential to harm – they have 'thing-power' (Bennett 2004). The objects in question were not autonomous entities but part of a wider assemblage of mobility: for the terrorist plot to succeed the objects had to firstly be chosen and altered, secreted onto the aircraft in hand luggage and by definition parasite the mobilities of transnational air routes.

In this chapter, I will address the role played by such objects in the constitution of specific mobilities and consider the place of objects in smuggling practices, particularly narcotics and tobacco smuggling. Just as the utilization of common artefacts of global travel demonstrates the complexity of contemporary material culture, smuggling practices also represent a decidedly heterogeneous conception of mobility (Turnbull 2000). Scholars investigating the economics and geopolitics of drug smuggling suggest that the separation between legal and illegal trade is not as straightforward as one may assume. Bhattacharyya (2005: 1) outlines the 'tangled interconnections' between legal and illegal trade, whose techniques and practices are inter-related. Forms of marginal capital are organized according to a set of economic and spatial practices that are parallel to legitimated forms of international trade. Even though there are clear divergences in the geographies of smuggling the aim here is to posit the *object-oriented* geographies of smuggling: the centrality of objects to spatial relations and illicit practices. I will investigate the implications for the status of the mundane object: those objects which form a backdrop to the everyday, but ones which also foster a more complex understanding of the relationship between the de-territorialization of the global mobilities of people and things. Such things describe surreptitious 'alternative' mobilities and a re-territorialization of legitimacy strategies in the form of customs seizures and security screening.

Within the wider context of a 'new mobilities paradigm' (Sheller and Urry 2006), the differing registers of mobility, both licit and illicit, point to a diverse, variegated and entangled make-up of the mobilities assemblage. The geographies of interconnection that embody the networked supply chains of commodity distribution also form the infrastructure of smuggling. Nodes where forms of exchange occur such as container ports, ferry terminals or airports can become tactical sites of infiltration for the smuggling activities of organized crime gangs (SOCA 2009/10). Central to this claim are the interconnectedness of supply chains and the parasitic harnessing of the stability of the organizational forces required to facilitate interconnections. The material culture of smuggling is a core concern of the illicit movement of illegal goods.

The alternative mobilities of smuggling

Drawing from Celia Lury's (1997) 'objects of travel' the smuggler-object is typified by the use of altered, improvised spaces for the smuggling of illegal materials, such as narcotics or tobacco: these range from shipping containers, children's teddy bears, the false floor of a pick-up truck, luggage or the underside of van trailers. Such objects have become registers of socio-political contexts including organized crime, lost tax revenues or the exploitation of people. The movement of such objects is produced by a complex infrastructure of mobility, attesting to clashing mobilities whether sanctioned or non-sanctioned. The location of objects and practices for illicit means such as smuggling within legitimated mobilities describes a parasitic relationship in a complex mobilities assemblage. To speak of the orderings of sanctioned mobilities without the immanent presence of such turbulent disorderings is to present a somewhat limited conception of mobility (Urry 2000). The geographies of interconnection that smuggling practices harness and exploit describe the spatio-temporal deterritorialization of globalization.

As Cresswell (2010) has recently argued, the 'new mobilities paradigm' could be read, in effect, as the restatement of historical debates on the movement of people seen in migration theory or the spatial dimensions of trade routes seen in transport geography. A shift in the ontologies of movement is a result of technological development, as well as the socio-cultural activities of mobility more generally. Various constellations of mobility are bound up with the entanglements of how things or people move. Mobility is differentially produced, distributed and consumed, according to various modes of access, privilege and subversion (Cresswell 2010: 21). 'Official' mobilities such as commodity distribution, tourism or transport cannot be disengaged from the immanent presence of non-sanctioned mobilities. The threat posed, for example by the 2003 SARS epidemic, has been attributed to the connectivity of global mobilities (Harris Ali and Keil 2010). Differentially produced constellations form 'mobilities assemblages' (De Landa 2006;

Salter 2008) where a multiplicity of actors organize and interrupt movement. Forms of transgression and lawlessness populate such mobilities assemblages alongside legitimated movement. The global illegal drugs trade, for example, is intertwined in the geographies of legal trade through practices of smuggling and in a wider geopolitical sense. Processes of 'alternative' mobilities are 'common to many other forms of trade in an unequal world' (Bhattacharya 2005: 93). Historically, the licit and illicit movement of commodities occurred simultaneously, where 'smuggling remained central to the circulation of commodities and workers throughout the eighteenth century' (Rediker 1987: 72).

Smuggling embodies a diversity of practices that have their own economic and labour constellations. Narcotics and tobacco smuggling have specific politics and sets of practices although various forms of smuggling often operate alongside one another. Tobacco smuggling, for example, can occur in tandem to the illegal trade in alcohol and narcotics (HM Treasury/HM Revenue and Customs 2006: 6). In his account of the Anglo-American maritime world of the eighteenth century, Rediker considers how attitudes towards the smuggling of contraband were given 'broad public support' (Rediker 1987: 73) throughout the ports and cities of the north Atlantic, as they provided forms of economic stability.

Although there are obvious divergences in the practices of smuggling according to the specificities of geography and the materials being smuggled, what links its various forms is the distributive reach of smuggling via the interconnections of supply chains and its 'criminal logistics' (SOCA 2009/10: 2). Castells has acknowledged the configurations of drug smuggling into North America, noting the early use of human carriers through to the organization of a more formalized infrastructure such as aircraft landing strips in the Bahamas. Nevertheless:

> Many other ways were and are used, as seizures by customs officers increased: commercial airlines, cargo ships, personal couriers, cocaine hidden in legally exported merchandise (construction materials, glass panels, fruits, cans, clothing and so on), as well as, particularly in the 1990s, land transportation across the Mexico-US border.

(Castells 2000: 197)

Castells' observations make clear how the distribution of illicit narcotics is dependent on a firmly established supply chain often utilizing extant mobilities, such as the concealment of illicit goods in 'legally exported merchandise'. The smuggling of illegal tobacco takes place through a complex supply and distribution chain, such as in hidden floors built into shipping containers, the use of roll-on roll-off traffic on ferries, and low-cost airline routes. At one UK container port, it is estimated that such methods account for some 52 million cigarettes smuggled in 2006/07. One HMRC operation in 2003 at Luton Airport is reported to have intercepted 'fifty-one bags containing 700,000 cigarettes on two flights'

(HM Treasury/HM Revenue and Customs 2006: 21). The trade in illegal and counterfeit tobacco has become so large that the United Kingdom's HM Revenue and Customs has developed a strategy to tackle the distribution of such items.

Object symmetries

The interaction of variegated and competing practices of mobilities make up a complex mobilities assemblage. Recent work in a variety of disciplines, such as social and cultural geography (Anderson and Wylie 2009), design theory (Julier 2009), material culture (Hicks and Beaudry 2010) and political theory (Bennett 2004) has reconsidered the status of the object as a significant and powerful force in making and remaking the social world. Much of this work on the power of the object relates to actor network theory scholars and Bruno Latour's (1992) work in particular. The question of the aesthetic and socio-cultural significance of material culture is central to the field of design history and theory. Objects can define the social, the spatial and the temporal and through their ability to affect social dynamics. Human agency does not exist in isolation but is entangled amidst ties to material and non-material things.

The sheer ubiquity, abundance and mundanity of everyday objects make them harnessable as smuggler-objects. Michael (2003: 132) argues that mundane objects and technologies 'afford a sort of generic stability and this rests on their essential functionality'. Such things are characterized by 'their capacity to be unnoticed, to quietly mediate, that is reproduce, what have become the commonalities of everyday life' (Michael 2003: 128). This taken-for-granted nature of objects facilitates an understanding of how objects arbitrate socio-spatial relations where performance of the everyday is mediated by their proliferation. In spatio-temporal terms, the normalization of certain objects and practices facilitates mobility – some objects can travel well because of their ubiquity and routinization as familiar signifiers of everyday movement.

Latour (1987) offers a means of reading the various processes of stabilization via the concept of the 'black box'. Described as a 'conceptual mainstay in science studies' (Michael 2000:131) and beyond, 'black boxing' refers to the way in which various technologies, scientific practices, in addition to objects and ideas become stabilized or taken-for-granted as a result of their efficiency of operation. This can be ascribed to mundane objects: every time we turn on an electronic item we do not consider the internal technologies behind this action, instead we accept their efficacy. This process accounts for technical work becoming 'invisible by its own success' (Latour 1999: 304) where stabilization serves to mask or conceal the time and effort that produces mundane objects. The stability, ubiquity and capacity to act or perform effectively enable the 'black box' to function as invisible and we do not feel obliged to question 'the massive network of alliances of which it is composed' (Harman 2009: 34). 'Black boxing' also plays a fundamental role in the effective mass movement and distribution of things where the infrastructure of mobility can be described as a form of black box in its own right. For objects to move through the networks of mobility is dependent on their status as stabilized and firmly established parts of a network.

Object mobilities

Three categories of object have been developed by Lury (1997) that relate to the concept of the 'smuggler-object:' the 'traveller-object'; the 'tripper-object'; and the 'tourist-object'. 'Traveller-objects' are typified by their symbolic importance and ability to move where meaning is not eradicated, such as works of art and craft objects. Such objects are hermeneutically and ontologically stable because of the 'authenticated relationship to an original dwelling'. 'Tripper-objects'' meanings can become reconfigured through various contexts, 'especially by their final dwelling' (Lury 1997: 79), such as the home, the mantelpiece, the domestic collection and may include the tourist souvenir, found-objects, keepsakes and mementos or even consumer goods. Critical to the status of the tripper-object is the ability to reach the final point of residence whilst being open to interpretation and emotional projection. 'Tourist-objects' are engaged and determined by movement and 'located in mobility itself' (Franklin 2003: 111). Such objects are characterized by certain forms of global cosmopolitanism, which are located beyond the local but are designed specifically for the purpose of distribution and circulation, such as clothing, television programmes or global food stuffs. These different categorizations demonstrate the complexity of object mobilities. All three are interwoven in a reciprocal bond that highlights how their meaning is reliant on the ability to move, whilst the mobility of the object is itself governed by the meaning or status of the object. Like Serres' (1995: 15) conception of the world-object, they demonstrate the networked trajectories of objects.

Conceptualizing the smuggler-object

The smuggler-object can be positioned at the intersection of stability, mobility, taken-for-grantedness and invisibility. Such an object may be mundane in its outward appearance, bearing the hallmark of legitimated mobilities. However, central to the smuggler-object is the capacity to conceal its illegality. Although illegal, it embodies a complex set of material practices and performances that combine the sheer quantity of distributed commodities being shipped around the globe, alongside other mobile objects. It is conceivable to conceptualize the smuggler-object through a fourfold approach: firstly, through the harnessing of the extant stabilities of infrastructural geographies; secondly, via the functionality of mundane objects, particularly when one contemplates an extended notion of use-value as a capacity to act; thirdly, through the use of covert spaces or the alteration of the object to create such spaces in which illicit goods may be smuggled; and finally, the smuggler-object may be read in terms of the black-boxing process, primarily through the containment or invisibility offered by the mundane black-boxed object.

The supply chain geographies of legitimated goods are premised on the highly tuned organization of movement, likewise the movement of tourists and vehicles relies upon the infrastructural power to mobilize vast numbers of people and things. With the smuggler-object, it is possible to argue that the strategies of stabilization required to distribute people and things are the very ones that become harnessed through the infiltration of the legal mobility networks. Given this the very notion of stability becomes problematized by smuggling-practices, suggesting that stability can only be read through the lens of instability and destabilization.

In similar terms, the smuggler-objects effects a reconsideration of what certain objects do and how they perform their supposedly prescribed function. Again, the conception of function is destabilized through the smuggler-object. In its basic state, use-value may be situated as part of 'the utility of a thing' (Marx 1970: 44); however, as Marx argues this is transformed by its 'elevation' to commodity status and thus into the logic of exchange. Dant (2005: 16) discusses a problematic in Marx's distinction between use-value and exchange-value, arguing that Marx's conception of exchange-value as a more relational, or perhaps contingent, expression limits the potential of use-value. I take this to suggest that use-value is not simply fixed in its functional categorization, but rather function or purpose has wider social impact. Indeed, this is exemplified by the work of anthropologists on the post-consumption biographies of objects that narrate the shifting terrain of purpose (Kopytoff 1986). This attests to the notion of heterogeneous forms of purpose and artefactual recalcitrance (Bennett 2004), where there is a transformation of purpose beyond that of legitimated and prescribed notions of use – here the smuggler-object expands the conditionality of use-value.

There is in this conception of use an obvious correspondence between human-centred intent and the delegation of purpose to the smuggler-object. The implication is that mundane smuggler-objects are employed precisely because they afford a form of disguise through the ability to either utilize spaces within the object to secrete illicit materials or to produce a false space for the same purpose. The alteration process is an important one because it highlights the materiality of the object. In particular, the relationship between surface and volume, with the outer skin of the object made to appear as if it remains an 'innocent' commodity.

Appearance is critical to the successful functioning of the smuggler-object, in that it should not attract the attention of the securitized gaze. It is perhaps this function of the smuggler-object that is most critical. On the one hand, the smuggler-object appears to utilize or parasite the utter mundanity of everyday artefacts, such as children's toys, motor vehicles or luggage. The black-boxed ubiquity and invisibility of such things is central to the illicit movement of drugs or tobacco and the attempted circumvention of detection. The relationship with black boxing is a complex one: it is tempting to argue that the use of mundane objects for the purpose of smuggling is tantamount to tearing open the black box, revealing the internal working mechanisms. As Latour (1999: 182) has described, it is only when technical objects (or systems) break down or lose their efficiency that the internal aspects of the black box are revealed. Prior to this, the black-boxed object appears as a collective one, without the need to consider it anything other than an efficiently operating collective black box. However, when the object fails and the black box 'opened', the inner workings come under scrutiny, each of the constituent parts revealed as black boxes in their own right. Although this may be pushing the metaphor a little too far the opening of the mundane black box through the parasitism of smuggling reveals the internal workings, the individual black boxes of the mundane objects of mobility. In spite of this, the smuggler-object must retain the *appearance* of the collective black box that maintains invisibility, opacity and stability.

Conclusions

The smuggler-object exemplifies that perceivably 'innocent' objects have a deleterious potential. The literature of material culture concerning everyday artefacts testifies to Bennett's (2004: 349) argument concerning 'thing-power' and of 'fostering greater recognition of the agential powers of natural and artifactual things.' The mobility of mundane objects disguises processes of stabilization and destabilization across a variety of registers. The concept of the black box offers an opportunity to think through a range of issues, such as the stabilization of infrastructure and supply chains, the politics of invisibility in relation to the consequences of concealment, as well as the materiality and design of mundane objects.

References

Anderson, B. and Wylie, J. (2009), 'On Geography and Materiality', *Environment and Planning A*, 41: 2, pp. 318–335.

Bennett, J. (2004), 'The Force of Things: Steps Toward an Ecology of Matter', *Political Theory*, 32: 3, pp. 347–372.

Bhattacharyya, G. (2005), *Traffick: The Illicit Movement of People and Things*, London: Pluto Press.

Castells, M. (2000), *End of Millennium: The Information Age – Economy, Society and Culture: Vol 3*, Oxford: Blackwell.

Cresswell, T. (2010), 'Towards a Politics of Mobility', *Environment and Planning D: Society and Space*, 28, pp. 17–31.

Dant, T. (2005), *Materiality and Society*, Maidenhead: Open University Press

De Landa, M. (2006), *A New Philosophy of Society: Assemblage Theory and Social Complexity*, London: Continuum.

Franklin, A. (2003), 'Tourist Objects, Tourist Rituals', in *Tourism: An Introduction*, London: SAGE, pp. 97–135.

Harman, G. (2009), *Prince of Networks: Bruno Latour and Metaphysics*, Melbourne: Re.Press.

Harris Ali, S. and Keil, R. (2010), 'Securitizing Networked Flows: Infectious Diseases and Airports', in S. Graham (ed.), *Disrupted Cities: When Infrastructure Fails*, Abingdon: Routledge. pp. 97–110.

Hicks, D. and Beaudry, M.C. (eds) (2010), *The Oxford Handbook of Material Culture Studies*, Oxford: Oxford University Press.

HM Treasury/HM Revenue and Customs (2006), *New Responses to New Challenges: Reinforcing the Tackling Tobacco Smuggling Strategy*, Norwich: HMSO.

Julier, G. (2009), 'Value, Relationality and Unfinished Objects: Guy Julier Interview with Scott Lash and Celia Lury', in *Design and Culture*, 1, 1, pp.93-104.

Kopytoff, I. (1986), 'The Cultural Biography of Things: Commoditization as Process', in A. Appadurai (ed.), *The Social Life of Things: Commodities in Cultural Perspective*, Cambridge: Cambridge University Press, pp. 64–91.

Latour, B. (1987), *Science in Action*, Cambridge, MA: Harvard University Press.

Latour, B. (1992), 'Where are the Missing Masses? The Sociology of a Few Mundane Artifacts', W.E. Bijker and J. Law (eds), *Shaping Technology/Building Society: Studies in Sociotechnical Change*, Cambridge, MA: MIT Press, pp. 225–258..

Latour, B. (1999), *Pandora's Hope: Essays on the Reality of Science Studies*, Cambridge, MA: Harvard University Press.

Latour, B. (2005), *Reassembling the Social: An Introduction to Actor-Network-Theory*, Oxford: Oxford University Press.

Laville, S., Norton-Taylor, R. and Dodd, V. (2006), 'A Plot to Commit Murder on an Unimaginable Scale', *The Guardian*, http://www.guardian.co.uk/uk/2006/aug/11/politics.usa1. Accessed 26 August 2006.

Lury, C. (1997), 'The Objects of Travel', in C. Rojek and J. Urry (eds), *Touring Cultures: Transformations of Travel and Theory*, London: Routledge, pp. 75–95.

Marx, K. (1970) *Capital: Vol. 1*, London: Lawrence and Wishart.

Michael, M. (2000), *Reconnecting Culture, Technology and Nature: From Society to Heterogeneity*, London: Routledge.

Michael, M. (2003), 'Between the Mundane and the Exotic: Time for a different Sociotechnical Stuff', *Time & Society*, 12: 1, pp. 127–143.

Rediker, M. (1987), *Between the Devil and the Deep Blue Sea: Merchant Seamen, Pirates, and the Anglo-American Maritime World, 1700–1750*, Cambridge: Cambridge University Press.

Salter, M. (2008), 'Introduction: Airport Assemblage', in M. Salter (ed.), *Politics at the Airport*, Minneapolis: University of Minnesota Press, pp. ix–xix.

Serres, M. (1995), *The Natural Contract*, Ann Arbor: University of Michigan Press.

Sheller, M. and Urry, J. (2006), 'The New Mobilities Paradigm, *Environment and Planning A*, 38: 2, pp. 207–226.

Turnbull, D. (2000), *Masons, Tricksters and Cartographers: Comparative Studies in the Sociology of Scientific and Indigenous Knowledge*, London: Routledge

Urry, J. (2000), *Sociology Beyond Societies: Mobilities for the Twenty First Century*, London: Routledge.

Part III

Projected Utopias

Chapter 8

The Cruel Dialectic: On the Work of Nils Norman

T. J. Demos

Figure 1. Nils Norman, *The Contemporary Picturesque* (cover), 2001.
Courtesy: Nils Norman.

Flipping through *The Contemporary Picturesque*, the conceptualist book created by British artist Nils Norman in 2001, one finds no breathtakingly beautiful landscapes or idyllic scenes. Instead, we discover a typology of 'deterrent designs:' barriers, surfaces and seating devices specifically made to control certain kinds of public behaviour. For each type, there are multiple examples, photographed and described through captions. For 'Barriers,' there are barricades that direct pedestrians, metal gates that manage crowd circulation, guardrails that block public access, traffic bollards that guide automobile routes. For 'Surfaces,' the book offers metal impediments placed between escalators to prevent sliding, surface studs that hamper sitting, anti-climb paint, anti-vandal materials, areas like steps or sidewalks that are periodically watered down to thwart loitering. For 'Seats,' there are inhospitable bus-stop perching ledges, vandal-proof metal and stone benches, uncomfortable garden-style folding chairs. Terse captions explain that the seating designs are pragmatic but limit comfort to dissuade long periods of relaxation and to prevent sleeping: 'Minimal design bus stop: low-maintenance, vandal proof with token perching ledge for short-term leaning. An ingenious design deterrent offering little shelter from the elements at minimum cost.' Introducing this archive of disciplinary designs, worthy of Michel Foucault, or even the Marquis de Sade, Norman's analytical commentary notes that 'Contemporary street furniture and technologies of surveillance are the physical infrastructure, the outward signs of the training, regulation and correction of behaviour to be found on a new island in the "carceral Archipelago:" the modern city' (Norman 2001).

Reading through this study, a slim volume of below 40 pages, we learn that public space has undergone significant transformation in recent years. It has become a disciplinary zone of surveillance ruled by increasingly efficient technologies of bodily regulation, one connected to the simultaneous reduction of funding of public infrastructure and increased privatization. 'This obsession with physical security systems, and, collaterally, with the architectural policing of social boundaries, has become a zeitgeist of urban restructuring, a master narrative in the emerging built environment of the 1990s,' writes Mike Davis of similar developments in *City of Quartz*, his landmark study of what he calls 'Fortress L.A.' (Davis 1990: 223). Roughly ten years later, Norman proves Davis correct. More, he shows that this restructuring has been globalized, 'the modern city' of New York, London, Hamburg, Tel Aviv being the object of his analysis in *The Contemporary Picturesque*. Although this global transformation surely correlates with today's post-9/11 paranoid environment, the hypostasis of 'national security,' and efforts to 'secure the homeland,'

Figure 2. Nils Norman, *The Contemporary Picturesque*
(Pedestrian Traffic Bollards, Tel Aviv, Israel, 2001).
Courtesy: Nils Norman.

Norman's work in fact precedes it, showing that the militarized fortification of cities has been long in the making. The development of surveillance and systems of control is consequently becoming increasingly studied and its appearance in artistic discourse is noteworthy. Recent examples include: Tom Levin et al. (2002); and *Homeland* (Whitney Museum of American Art 2003), the catalog for the recent 2003 Whitney ISP exhibition, which, among other things, examined the relations between security and nationalism.

The Contemporary Picturesque excavates the prehistory of current developments in city design, locating their origins in nineteenth-century Paris and the urban restructuring that was Haussmannization. During that period of urbanization and population growth, Paris grew from a medieval town of small tortuous streets and tightly packed buildings into a cosmopolitan city organized by rationalized networks of grand boulevards, which became 'the panoptic spatial expression of control in city design,' as Norman notes in his introductory essay. He writes further:

> To stroll in the new cities of the 19th century was to encounter a society imposing and establishing new norms of behaviour and measures of delinquency. The process was in part a deliberate training and perhaps more importantly an internalization of new rules and expectations—in order that capital's accelerating flow of workers and goods could continue to develop, unhindered by excessive outbreaks of emancipation or solidarity around common causes.

(Norman 2001)

Figure 3. Nils Norman, *The Contemporary Picturesque*
(Bus Stop bench, Hamburg, 2001). Courtesy: Nils Norman.

Photographs of contemporary urban space detail how this 'training' and 'internalization of new rules and expectations' have advanced to the point of an architectural design specialization more than a century later. Panoptic systems have been tweaked, street furniture perfected, surveillance technologies ever improved. It appears that Foucault's (1979: 227, 217) earlier speculations about an eventual 'ideal point' of 'infinite discipline' in which 'the individual is carefully fabricated' is well on its way to being implemented.

Against a growing number of photographers who tend to beautify the current globalized conditions of public space, through dramatic compositions, saturated colours, digital processing and high-quality, large-scale prints (e.g. Andreas Gursky), Norman's images are decidedly anti-aesthetic. Mostly black-and-white documentary shots, presented in a book, they simply and directly focus on their subjects without flourish or compositional artistry. The photograph of 'surface studs', for instance, provides a close-up view of a marble ledge punctuated with steel points. Uniformly in focus, shot at an oblique angle, the image merely serves to provide visual information efficiently. Pedantically, a curt caption is added: 'Upmarket metal studs on marble prevent people from sitting on private property and add a perverse yet strangely apt S&M flavour to the City's streets.' Or, another photograph shows a man watering public steps to prevent loitering in front of a store. A wider frame is employed to show the full expanse of the surface area. Nondescript and banal, it obeys the law of maximum legibility. If such photographs constitute our 'contemporary picturesque', then this phrase suggests a tragic-comic characterization that exploits the difference between the ideal and the actual by reversing the terms, best described as ironic. On the one hand, Norman's use of picturesque invokes a state of ideal beauty, but only to sarcastically cast into relief the depressing reality that has turned urban space into a zone of discipline and punishment. On the other hand, it parodies the contemporary art that transforms such scenes of domination into visual delectation, such as the ever-increasing monumentalized photographs that beautify architectures of consumerism or spaces of social inequality, making them into sublime typologies of masochistic desire rather than fostering critical viewpoints. Peter Galassi (2001: 26) compares Gursky's photographs, for example, to 'Friedrich's sublime interventions', if not to the picturesque.

In contrast, Norman resuscitates older conceptual art lineages to explore how public space has been fractured by conflicting interests and to invoke representational strategies to rupture the seeming ineluctability of those conditions. Like the art of Allan Sekula or Martha Rosler, his photography and text format is heterogeneous, breaking down the referent of pubic space into its discursive conditions, political determinations and historical genealogies. Norman's artistic activism also invokes the oppositional artistic practices of Hans Haacke and Krzysztof Wodiczko that contest the supposed neutrality of space in favour of revealing its political and economic conditions. If Norman's typological model also recalls elements of conceptual photography, it resembles less that of the Bechers' careful and aestheticizing views of industrial architectures and more to the deadpan and amateur delivery of Ed Ruscha's photo books. Not surprisingly, Norman

Figure 4. Nils Norman, *The Contemporary Picturesque*
(Surface Studs, City of London, 2001). Courtesy: Nils Norman.

takes his own images and derives them from public image archives, refusing to locate his artistic signature in the technical practice of photography. Similarly, he references a wide array of urban studies and historical accounts of public space in his text. Norman's work thereby diversifies authorial agency, which prevents the fetishization of an individual photographic style or single artist's voice. The focus, instead, is on the critical (and implicitly collaborative) examination of disciplinary mechanisms at work in public space.

However, although the need for such a critical project seems more urgent now than ever, one detects an unmistakable humour in *The Contemporary Picturesque*; a tongue-in-cheek intonation that brings levity to its voice and distances its presentation from those of earlier artistic models. Often self-directed, Norman's irony is not easy to pin down: is it the perfunctory seriousness with which his analysis is undertaken, with all the appropriate nods to conceptual art and urban studies, paralleled by the ludicrous nature of its objects of study? Is it the sarcastic suggestion that today's counterparts to Poussin and Claude, the original painters of the picturesque, are the petty designers of manipulative street furniture? Or could it be the absurdist gesture of proposing a new front for activist energies, one that would protest the emergence of inhospitable bus seats and manipulative guardrails? (Yet, the book seems to compel just that when it shows the sadistically oppressive design of public space) If it becomes clear that it is difficult to consider *The Contemporary Picturesque* as a new model of activist art, then what ends does its irony serve?

The new picturesque

Robert Smithson's study of Olmsted's 'picturesque' Central Park, appearing in *Artforum* in 1973, was one point of departure for Norman's project. Smithson's 1973 essay, 'Frederick Law Olmsted and the Dialectical Landscape,' employs the term 'picturesque' as a way to de-idealize the landscape, even if this appears counter-intuitive. But rather than drawing on the familiar connotations of the picturesque, which suggest some immutable appearance or idealized static identity, Smithson found in it a way to stress the landscape's location within an intertwined network of abstract representations, shifting temporal conditions and multiple social uses. To backtrack, Smithson wished to develop within his own artistic practice a revisionary understanding of the landscape to escape from 'the spiritualism of Thoreauian transcendentalism,' and, more immediate to his context in the early1970s, from its offspring, the lingering '"modernist formalism" rooted in Kant, Hegel and Fichte.' Those authors saw nature as 'a thing-in-itself' rather than 'a process of ongoing relationships existing in a physical region…a 'thing-for-us.' (Smithson 1996: 160). This tendency began much earlier, noted Smithson, with Edmund Burke's *Inquiry in the Origin of Our Ideas of the Sublime and the Beautiful*, 1757, which posited a 'dialectic' between the 'beautiful' and the 'sublime' – the former signifying qualities such as smoothness, gentle curves and natural delicacy; the latter terror, solitude, and vastness. Both were rooted in the real world rather than in a Hegelian ideal realm. Moving into the later-eighteenth and early nineteenth centuries, Uvedale Price and William Gilpin pushed Burke's theory further, synthesizing his terms in a new descriptor: the 'picturesque'. Smithson argued that the heterogeneity suggested in this word and evident in its history, provided a way to defeat static understandings of the landscape. The picturesque emphasized the processes of chance and change in the material order of nature. If a 'dialectical landscape', then its 'dialectic' was meant to refer to an irrevocable state of conflict built of internal differences rather than a sublated unity. And because it necessitates active interpretation and ongoing conceptual negotiation, the picturesque would reclaim the landscape as a 'thing-for-us' rather than reflecting some idealist self-enclosed entity given over to us.

New York City's Central Park was a case in point. 'Olmsted's parks', Smithson noted, 'exist before they are finished, which means in fact they are never finished; they remain carriers of the unexpected and of contradiction on all levels of human activity, be it social, political or natural' (Smithson 1996: 160). Smithson's photographs stress this heterogeneity, eliciting the landscape's dialectic. They capture Central Park in extraordinary moments of physical transition, existing through and between different historical periods and disparate spaces. Focusing on one area behind the Metropolitan Museum of Art, perfectly exemplifying the landscape in formation by placing the exemplary space of idealism in the context of lived reality, one photograph from his essay shows a wall marked up with graffiti, situated between nature and a construction site, where 'nature' and 'construction' are thrown into productive confusion. Revealed as a zone of social, political and natural conflict, the scene emphasizes a landscape composed of images within images. Photography's own doubleness as a reproductive technology opens up the landscape's multiplicity. For critic Craig Owens, this reveals the mise-en-abyme of Smithson's photography, where 'reality itself appears to be already constituted by an image'(Owens 1992: 27). Consequently, photography's representational structure becomes 'allegorical', occurring 'whenever one text is doubled by another', as Owens (1992: 53) defined it.

The publication of Smithson's essay in *Artforum* also rendered his portrayal allegorical, pushing it further into a labyrinth of 'sites' and 'non-sites', the artist's terms for the inextricable relation between geography and its representations. The essay submitted the landscape to additional doublings and recodings, now in the act of its dissemination. Smithson frequently played off the inevitable redefinition of the site that resulted when this representational mobilization occurred. And he often ironized this structure of discursive mimesis (when the object or site gives itself over to the conventions of its distribution of form), as when he presented and narrated a slide show of the run-down hotel, *Hotel Palenque* in Mexico, as if it were an important pre-Columbian archeological site (1969). Or when he conspicuously termed dilapidated industrial machinery and discarded piping in Passaic, New Jersey, 'monuments', as if they were of art-historical importance (*The Monuments of Passaic*, 1967, also published

Figure 5. Robert Smithson, Central Park, 1972.

in *Artforum*). The irony of these gestures is palpable, though Smithson seemed to draw on its less derisive sense, merely producing a rhetorical incongruity between apparent and intended meanings.

A variant of the allegorical, irony defined by the *Oxford English Dictionary* (1971: 484) as 'a figure of speech in which the intended meaning is the opposite of that expressed by the words used; usually taking the form of sarcasm or ridicule in which laudatory expressions are used to imply condemnation or contempt,' opens a breach within language, inviting an often comic discrepancy between different senses, as if placing a signifier in quotation marks and encouraging its contextual play. Owens suggests that 'it should be remembered that irony itself is regularly enlisted as a variant of the allegorical; that words can be used to signify their opposites is in itself a fundamentally allegorical perception.' Owens (1992: 61–62). Etymologically, the root of allegory is the

Greek *allegoria*, meaning 'to speak as to imply something other'. *Eironeia*, from *eiron*, the Greek root of irony, means 'feigned ignorance'. In Smithson's case, the emphasis on the doubleness of language reveals how different forms of discourse could play a role in the reframing of unexpected objects like the run-down Hotel Palenque or the 'The Great Pipe Monument' in Passaic when submitted to an ironic delivery. And the result would subsequently reflect critically on its own representational conventions, like the art-history lecture or the magazine article, in Smithson's cases, as well as give a new perspective to their represented objects.

Smithson's 'dialectic of place' prepared the ground for Norman's book project in that it exposed 'reality' as being far from natural or unified (as conservative understandings of the picturesque would have it) but instead traversed by ideological layers and contradictory representations. In fact, while teaching in New York recently, Norman revisited the sites of Smithson's study with a group of students. Also, Smithson provided an artistic strategy that would erode the reification of public space by revealing its picturesque heterogeneity through a complex representational system. Consequently, urban space was exposed as a conflicted socio-political field, also a goal of Norman's project. Norman's work develops this de-idealizing view and specifies how the 'picturesque' operates today: 'as an important tool of gentrification'. Referencing Smithson, Norman's text explains that

Central Park is now more picturesque than Olmsted could ever have hoped for. Tomkins Square park [in the East Village] has been redesigned so that it is more panoptic in form; it has a strict, police-patrolled curfew and its walkways have been widened to two police car widths. Herald Square [in Midtown] has two triangular-shaped parks, both in a distinctly Haussmannesque style with extra wide walkways, curfews, private guards and a token sprinkling of low maintenance shrubbery.

(Interview with Jennifer Allen, 'Utopia Now: The Art of Nils Norman', January 2002, available from http://www.artforum.com)

Additionally, we can trace back to Smithson the ironic structure that is evident in Norman's work, which informs Norman's double-edged tone. This doubleness unfolds from the duplicitous model that is *The Contemporary Picturesque*: on the one hand, the book references conceptual art models, such as the photo-typologies of Ruscha and the visual–textual systems of Smithson; but on the other hand, it mimics the very tourist guidebooks and commercial urban-planning brochures that helped have define the picturesque for commercial purposes such as the *Street Furniture Manual* (Westminster City: Planning and Transportation Department, 1993), cited in *The Contemporary Picturesque*. This latter mimicry is clear in the modish design of the book, the sometimes glossy illustrations and clichéd captions, as well as in its language, which seems to alternate between critique and advertisement ('Minimal design…at minimum cost'). Yet, how do such models interact when melded together? If conceptual art paradigms of criticality are meant to subvert commercial design, what happens when this strategy backfires and the two models merge or is that the point? What is gained when the book speaks out of both sides of its mouth? And more broadly, what is the relevance and value of such ironic gestures for contemporary artistic practice?

Critical practices

While the doubleness at work in Norman's project surely satirizes the 'contemporary picturesque', meaning here the disciplinary public space and the urban-planning brochures that reproduce it, a further effect is that it distances itself from the very forms of criticality it invokes. This complication appears to be a result of the inevitable doubt with which one approaches any supposedly subversive model of artistic activity today in the wake of the seeming failures of critical art in the past, a scepticism already apparent in Smithson's project forty years ago. And it seems to acknowledge the consistent inability of advanced art to halt, or even slow, the growth of globalized corporate hegemony, let alone the voracious appetite of the real estate industry. For when art tries to do so, we witness the seemingly inevitable conversion of critique into affirmation, identified by Benjamin Buchloh (1990: 140) as the 'major paradox of all conceptual practices,' now some forty years old: 'that the critical annihilation of cultural conventions itself immediately acquires the conditions of the spectacle, that the … demolition of authorship produces instant brand names and identifiable products, and that the campaign to critique conventions of visuality…inevitably ends by following the pre-established mechanisms of advertising and marketing campaigns.' If true, then how can such critical practices be credibly resuscitated today *without* a sense of scepticism and doubt?

Or, consider Fredric Jameson's view of the modern transformation of the sublime, which forms part of the picturesque. For Jameson, the sublime was once expressed in Modernism's search for an Absolute that stood outside of capitalism's popular culture of consumerism. This autonomous zone of negativity, wherein avant-garde practice was once purportedly located, has gradually disappeared in what Jameson refers to as the 'postmodern' era. Instead, the 'Beautiful' – the other half of the picturesque – has become ascendant, but is now fused with commercialism: 'the return of the Beautiful must be seen as just such a systematic dominant: a colonization of reality generally by spatial and visual forms which is at one and the same time a commodification of that same intensively colonized reality on a world-wide scale' (Jameson 2000: 87). If the sublime once existed in the modern period, when it coincided with modernism, then it offered a space bulwarked against commodification; that is, until the distinction between the two collapsed under the pressure of late capitalism. Accordingly, we now face a world order where, according to Jameson, everything visible is acculturated and everything acculturated, commodified. One consequence is that we meet the end of the 'aesthetic' as such, where all 'traditional distinctiveness or 'specificity' of the aesthetic (and even of culture as such) is necessarily blurred or lost altogether' (Jameson 2000: 111). A second result is that today, when the image is thoroughly consolidated into the commodity form, contemporary 'pseudo-aestheticism' is revealed to be an ideological manoeuvre and can no longer function as a creative resource. All beauty, Jameson concludes, is now meretricious.

Far from unaware of these developments, Norman's practice elaborates on them and stealthily operates within their terms. From his book, we gain an idea of how the 'picturesque', Jameson's 'beautiful' in humorous reversal, is often composed out of the ruins of past avant-garde forms, specifically in terms of the complicity of its aesthetic with commercial design. This occurs in two ways: in the design and representation of public space. In terms of design, what is surprising in Norman's photographs is that the deterrent forms appearing within them paradoxically resemble 'minimal designs', to use Norman's term, whether as a modular surface of pyramidal mouldings built into the ground to make sitting uncomfortable, which recalls so many floor sculptures of Carl André, or as the repetitive structure of an industrial steel gate that directs traffic that brings to mind Donald Judd's minimalist objects. Once offering an aesthetic of negation against the encroachment of the commodity form, minimalism's serial structures and monochromatic surfaces now find themselves employed as vehicles to facilitate consumerism. Minimalism has also become a tool of urban discipline, its negativity reversing into instrumentalization, its anti-anthropomorphism becoming urban design's sadism. If minimalist structures once provided complex spaces of perceptual critique and offered ideal possibilities for phenomenological self-consciousness, they are now directed against the public body, transmogrifying into a logic of 'defensible space' and psychosomatic manipulation, a phrase coined by Oscar Newman (1972) in the early 1970s to designate urban design as crime prevention. Newman describes 'real and symbolic barriers, strongly defined areas of influence and improved opportunities for surveillance that combine to bring an environment under the control of its residents.' (Newman, 1972: 3). If post-minimalism later attempted to make one aware of the deep socio-political fissures in public space and in the constitution of the 'public' by materializing spatial divisions through the use of large-scale sculptural interventions (most famously in Richard Serra's *Tilted Arc*, 1981), today's deterrent designs increasingly relegate the 'public' to the class of consumers. Moreover, they work to purify the public by eliminating all undesirables: to keep the vagrant body away from all areas, off surfaces, regulated when seated, controlled when walking, all in the name of reproducing an ideal consumerized subject. Once considered emancipatory, minimalism is now channelled under the sign of the spectacle, colonizing reality on a global scale even while serving as the perverse decoration of public space.

Norman's exposure of this 'contemporary picturesque' state is not unique. A precedent exists in Dan Graham's work of the 1960s, specifically his dry photographs of 'minimalist' urban spaces, such as those contained in his magazine project, *Homes for America* (1966), which located modular structures in the repetitive architecture of mass-produced housing.

As a result, minimalism's claims to autonomy and criticality were seen to be jeopardized. Additionally, by enveloping his own 'art object' within its commercial distribution system, publishing *Homes for America* in the pages of *Art in America*, a mass-produced art magazine, Graham, like Smithson, showed art to be inevitably recoded by commercial institutions. Norman's work is doubly indebted in this regard: first, it similarly examines the commercial instrumentalization of minimalism even though it updates the analysis by revealing the perversity of minimalism's reappearance in the guise of disciplinary design (here connecting with Graham's own investigations into surveillance and the visuality of corporate architecture); and second, Norman's representational model based on commercial design booklets internalizes, like Graham's, the very format of its target of critique (a move I will consider further below).

Figure 6. Nils Norman, *The Contemporary Picturesque*
(Studded Paving, Kings Cross, London, 2001). Courtesy: Nils Norman.

Norman's is of course not the only contemporary practice to have examined this 'perverse' legacy of minimalism. Similar is Tom Burr's *Palm Beach Views* of 1999, a series of photographs that shows images of landscape hedges that resemble minimalist objects but which have been put to disciplinary purpose. Considering Burr's use of photography and text, the series also invokes the work of Smithson and Graham, and his project deploys an ironic documentary mode as well. Burr photographed what he calls 'anti-public' landscape designs, hedges cut into minimalist geometries, strategically grown to segregate and protect the private property of wealthy gated communities. The photographic viewpoints are deadpan, revealing intransigent façades that ridiculously obscure the architecture they guard. In the short text that accompanies the photos, Burr unravels an allegory of imagined transgression within the hedges, connecting their spaces

Figure 7. Tom Burr, *Palm Beach Views*, 1999.

to his sculptural projects (such as *Deep Purple*, 2000, a work that plays on Smithson's *Tilted Arc*). His tales reclaim in fiction not only the liminal space of the hedges but also the erotic allure of minimalism, evoked through his subjective reframing (Burr 2000: 18–19). Such artistic practice doubles back on the work of preceding generations, wrestling artistic models away from their commercial appropriations, rendering minimalism's perversion by design perverse in turn. But if Burr's project, like Norman's, functions critically, it also reads at times as absurdist – but with a point. Simultaneously, this art attacks not only its targeted object (urban design or suburban landscaping) for its abuses of the avant-garde; it also reflexively revisits its own artistic form, self-consciously complicating its own mode of transmission.

Strategies of space

Such twists also appear in other works of Norman, such as *Edible Playscape Bristol*, a related project of 2001 that documents a public square in the South Western English city. For that Norman created a poster that shows various photographic views of St. James Barton Roundabout, a dilapidated urban area marked for gentrification. The views portray the existent deterrent designs, barren walkways and the depressing landscaping of the roundabout; others show the predatory billboards of the real estate industry advertising the first stages of redevelopment – the conversion of post-industrial spaces into luxury lofts. Texts, interspersed throughout the poster, further reveal this logic: 'The physical deterioration and economic devalorisation of inner-city neighbourhoods is a strictly logical, rational outcome of the operation of the land and housing markets,' reads one caption, quoting the geographer Neil Smith (2000). Others identify a common strategy of gentrification once the process of planned devalorization is complete: the 'theme-ing' of public space, whereby romantic and nostalgic associations (e.g. from Bristol's maritime past) are cast over target areas to market them as alluring for the 'pioneers' of redevelopment. In such cases 'History becomes a cliché,' as the poster informs us. As a result of this presentation, the roundabout is revealed as a structural object of disciplinary urban planning, gentrification and profiteering.

The Bristol poster departs from the single-frame images that characterize *The Contemporary Picturesque*. Instead, it presents a model of photomontage updated through digital technology. Variously sized images stand next to or under adjacent fields of text, some pixilated staggered with reduced captions, constituting a slick surface of eye-catching forms, dynamic and asymmetrical. If this is photography's *mise-en-abyme*, opening up Bristol's public space to critical allegory, to a dialectic of images within images, the surface also tends to congeal into a seamless digital continuum. In many ways, this photomontage is less avant-gardist than advertisement or infomercial, less fissured materiality than smoothly assembled and printed image. It appears as a self-conscious take-off of recent innovations in commercial design (calling to mind, for instance, models

Figure 8. Nils Norman, *Edible Playscape, Bristol*, 2001.
Front view. Courtesy: Nils Norman.

such as the Zone Books of Bruce Mau Design, and Rem Koolhaas's catalogue, *S,M,L,XL*). Like *The Contemporary Picturesque*, the Bristol poster paradoxically combines critical and consumerist modes of representation, but to what end? If 'the central proposition [of design] involves erasing the boundaries between architecture and information, the real and the virtual,' as Mau (2000: 24) claims, then this also divulges the strategy behind the theme-ing of public spaces such as Bristol's square: turning architecture into information allows the easy manipulation of the real via the virtual. Art historian Hal Foster identifies the commercial value of such an erasure of boundaries: 'Today it has reached the point where not only commodity and sign appear as one, but often so do commodity and space: in actual and virtual malls the two are melded through design' Foster 2002: 23).

Norman's poster captures this very absorption of public space by urban design at the level of graphic spectacle. By mimicking the packaging of public space in urban planners' visual materials, real estate advertisements and designer handouts (some of the models Norman acknowledges using), the poster mimics the ways in which design – as the commercial progeny of avant-garde photomontage – has transformed public space into a virtual realm of manipulation. It shows that the disciplinary transformation of real space is paralleled by the commodification of its representational space. Increasingly collapsed together, each is equally designed for and by private interests. While the poster morphs the ruins of avant-garde photomontage into the digitized currency of commercial graphics, it also dramatizes the contrast between the decaying urban areas it represents and the poster's glossy surface. The move is not only mimetic but critical. While the poster reveals once again the termination of modernist negation in the accommodation of capitalism (although avant-garde photomontage was long ago appropriated as advertisement or instrumentalized as propaganda), Norman only begins with this acknowledgment and then attempts to carve out critical space in its aftermath. In the process, the poster uses design procedures to expose the economic cycle of decay and renewal by focusing on run-down public areas at the moment when the process of gentrification begins – when dilapidated space is metamorphosed into the high-finished surface that his poster internalizes. If texts are interspersed within the montage, they attempt to open up the image, rupturing its seduction, interrupting its visual field with critical analysis and historical content. Here, the poster puts design strategies to subversive ends: to spread unconventional information, to educate the public about the plans and tactics of the real estate industry, and to reveal the machinations in the urban planning of Bristol. Additionally, when displayed at Bristol's Arnolfini gallery, posters were stacked on a plinth and freely available, invoking a model of distribution split between conceptualist lineages and real estate industry marketing procedures. Its free accessibility (recalling the stack pieces of Felix Gonzales-Torres) challenged the privatization of Bristol's public space.

Conversely, the poster's design also indicates the degree to which any oppositional content is liable to be spectacularized itself. In fact, part of the point of Norman's work – and the very function of its irony – seems to be reflecting on the compromised status of criticality today. This explains, perhaps, why its texts, even though freighted with radical content, appear to degenerate into slogans themselves, especially within their reified surface. Decontextualized, they float in space, taking on an ambiguous relation to the photographs that appear next to or under them. Absorbed into a sound-bite model of communication, they become vulnerable to the consumerist habits that increasingly infect viewing conditions today. 'History becomes a cliché,' indeed. The inevitable limitations of artistic models that would be politically subversive become reflexively identified in Norman's work, which distances itself from its own critical agenda even while advancing it. A critique of gentrification is offered and criticality's collapse into spectacle is exposed. Is this yet another dialectical landscape, of geographical sites, conflictual representations, contradictory conventions and oppositional forces that is opened up to view, even though it all paradoxically coalesces into a single over-determined articulation? Its ironic distance from itself, from the models it employs, signals that there is more here than what meets the eye. Another way to look at it, however, is to see its irony as not only producing cynical conclusions but also creating productive possibilities , such as advancing critique without the self-assuredness and triumphalism of avant-garde models.

Public space

The counterpart to Norman's critical work is his series of utopian 'Proposals'. Made out of computer-generated diagrams and small-scale three-dimensional models, they suggest ideal ways to redesign parks, museums and other existing public spaces. They include emancipatory architectures, the utilization of ecologies based on renewable energies and sustainable resources, and the promotion of radical forms of democratic organization. Exemplary is the proposal printed on the other side of the Bristol poster, where its utopian proposal becomes the reverse of its documented reality – or reality, utopia's dark underside. The redesigned Bristol square is renamed *The Edible Forest Garden Park and Monument to Civil Disobedience Adventure Playground, St. James Barton Roundabout, Bristol*, the image of which entices us with its propositions for an inclusive and egalitarian public area with environmentally sensitive gardens and politically correct monuments. Rendered as a mostly green island, it appears in perspective, set against a light blue background, with texts surrounding the diagrams and placed in bubbles that mimic the circular shape of the garden. Gone is the sharp rectilinearity that defines the other side of the poster and a colourful digital illustration replaces documentary photomontage. The imagined park is filled with several community gardens, where fruit trees and vegetables are grown for public consumption. There is space for a farmer's market and a wildlife sanctuary. Captions describe it further: 'the park is made into a "Commons,"' owned and maintained by the people of Bristol preventing development by corporate and private interests.' Countering gentrification, deterrent designs and privatization, the *Playground* redirects the roundabout so that it privileges 'equal opportunities, social justice, inclusion of disadvantaged people and a strong commitment to sustainable development.'

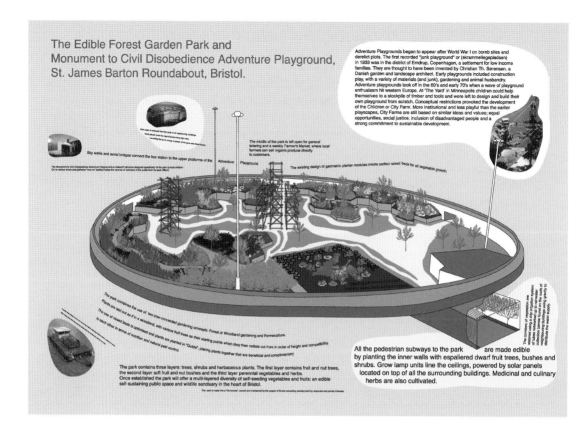

Figure 9. Nils Norman, *Edible Playscape, Bristol*, 2001.
Back view. Courtesy: Nils Norman.

Norman's proposals suggest, in a way, a critique of critique, implying that the subversion of existing discourses and practices is today insufficient. They answer the spectacularization of negation (revealed in his photography) with the need for something constructive. This aspect is important because it signals the fact that Norman's project moves beyond artistic models of the 1980s and 1990s that focused on negation without proposing alternatives (Joselit 2003: 3–14). But if the proposals turn away from these critical models, they resonate with other avant-garde precedents, calling up various utopian practices from Soviet constructivism to the Situationists. For example, some evoke constructivist kiosks and pavilions (consider Norman's *Proposal 14* of 1999, called 'a small children's rights and anti-patriarchy non-violent direct action kiosk'); others recall Soviet agitprop vehicles such as trains and ships (redeployed in Norman's *Geocruiser bus* of 2001). *The Bristol Playground* parallels projects such as Konstantin

Melnikov's *Plan for the Green City* of 1929. Schematized in a circular diagram using text and pictograms, the plan envisions an island of ideal life, offering a collectivist retreat for the regeneration of the urban proletariat, industrialized and exhausted. The *Green City* would offer gardens and a forest for sunlight and fresh air, including solar pavilions to concentrate the sun's rays on pallid faces. When outside, visitors would be able to reunite with an idealized nature where wild animals roamed freely. A 'Laboratory of Sleep,' utilizing every available technology, would ensure workers' rest, and the city's energy would be drawn from the wind (Starr 1978). In other respects, Norman's *Playground*,

Figure 10. Konstantin Melnikov, *Solar Pavilion for the Green City*, 1929.

particularly its scaffolding structures, sky walks and aerial bridges, brings to mind the work of Situationist urbanist Constant Nieuwenhuys. Norman's frequent use of such elements, designed for civil-disobedience training or to ensure means of circulation and escape from the police (although it is unclear, at least at this point, why one would need to escape from utopia), suggest forms of de-territorialization and autonomy also found in the playscapes of Constant, particularly his models and diagrams for *New Babylon*, 1959–74. Constant's futuristic architectures were meant to encourage emancipatory ways of inhabiting space, ludic behaviour through endless derives, once labour was outmoded, as utopians believed it would be by advancing technology (Wigley 1998).

But if Norman's proposals are designated as 'utopian' gestures (he uses the term himself to describe them) then, unlike these avant-garde precedents, they emphasize the impossibility that is written into the very term utopia as a 'non-place'. In fact, as Louis Marin (1984) points out, the term utopia, from the Greek *oú-topos*, 'no-place', and *eú-topos*, 'place of happiness', has negativity built into itself grammatically. Norman's utopian proposals announce such impossibility, first of all, in the typical multiplicity of their references: if they point to avant-garde genealogies, they also call up pop-cultural representations, such as the assembly directions for Ikea products or the 'imagineered' designs of Disney parks. Additionally, when Norman builds his three-dimensional models (a photograph of one is shown in upper right of the Bristol Playground), he uses HO-scale materials commonly used by design firms in the popularizing and marketing of their projects. But this conflation of avant-garde models and pop-cultural designs is not simply a matter of appearance. *The Bristol Playground* is as much an architecture of 'reassurance' as any Disney formula (Marling 1997). Both reduce the complexity of socio-political-environmental crises to cartoon-like solutions. Just how, for example, will the Bristol proposal achieve 'social justice?' The phrase reads as empty (perhaps that is why escape is necessary).

In concentrating these contradictory meanings into a single surface, Norman suggests various connections among them, creating another 'dialectical landscape'. But if we witness the conjunction of utopian programs with present-day spectacle, then this is less comparative than genealogical. There are of course numerous reasons to consider why such utopian dreamworlds have ended in catastrophe (Buck-Morss 2000). The great Soviet experiment, for instance, eventually spiralled downward into oppressive Stalinist domination, whereas the revolutionary hopes of the 1960s were realized as industrialized leisure and marketed lifestyles or as the non-spaces of mass public banality. Martha Rosler's *Airport Series* perfectly captures one such trajectory of this degeneration of constructivism into dystopia by discovering the perverted legacy of Constant's *New Babylon* and other avant-garde strategies in current conditions.

The utopian dream of architecture, removed from the spaces of daily life, was fastened onto nowheresville airportland, a controlled city space that is a cousin to the false fronts of new (sub)urbanism, another incarnation of gated, and policed, sites of habitation.

Figure 11. Constant, *Orange Construction*, 1958.

The minimalism of such spaces, which appear to answer to the disjunct needs of modern transit and commerce, mutely promise the giant empty room that Adorno and others used as the presiding metaphor of the modern surveillance society—the society of total administration.

(Rosler 2001: 128)

However, if Norman's proposals recognize the difficulty in articulating their utopian promise outside of their commercial appropriation, the artist still tries: he explains that 'resuscitating previous experimental corpses, largely perceived as failures or embarrassingly dated modes of thinking, is a deliberate route chosen for re-accessing dimensions of memory and history discarded by the market' (Norman 2002: 71). Such a path avoids the over-powering sense of nostalgia and melancholy that are the common side-effects of allegory by refusing to collapse the loss of the dream into the historical failures of its realization. Susan Buck-Morss captures a similar aim in her following recommendation: 'we … would do well to bring the ruins up close and work our way through the rubble in order to rescue the utopian hopes that modernity engendered, because we cannot afford to let them disappear' (Buck-Morss 2000: 68).

Yet, if Norman's utopian proposals reveal their impossibility by invoking the systems of co-optation that have rendered them unlikely, they are not impossible because of any technological reasons: Permaculture is available, alternative fuel is feasible, solar energy is operational, democratic forms of organizing society are not unknown. This is

Figure 12: Martha Rosler, *Untitled (JFK)*, 1999.
Courtesy: Martha Rosler.

a critical point: Norman's projects *could* be built but *are not*: they are within grasp but go unrealized. Norman's use of 'utopia' exposes the degree to which the utopian itself has been colonized, such that even those desires to change reality in ways that are possible are consigned to a zone of fiction. Labelling something as utopian appears as an easy way to dismiss unconventional ideas and in the process, imagination itself is shut down, either as a result of feared accusations of being unrealistic or through the inability to imagine change. Such has long been the case. Adorno long ago suggested that the derogatory use of the utopian functioned to resolve tensions between the possibilities of change and their extreme difficulties, or their impossibility in certain ways, the result being that one chooses the impossible to surrender unorthodox thinking. The outcome, in effect, is to masochistically identify with the aggressor: 'saying this should not be, whereby they feel that it is precisely this that should be' (Bloch 1986: 4). Norman's work points to other factors besides technological reasons that make his proposals unlikely, if not impossible: the powerful structures of private interests that enforce a disciplinary regime in public areas; the domination of the profit mechanism over all else; the systemic reproduction of regular cycles of dilapidation and gentrification; governmental bodies vulnerable to the influence of corporate power; the training of the 'public' as a homogeneous mass of consumers; and so on. Norman's use of the utopian, in other words, is far from escapist; it critically reflects back on reality.

It is consequently not surprising to learn that his proposals are not *meant* to be realized, contrary to those commentaries that have critiqued his work for existing only at the hypothetical level. As Norman explains:

> My main use of utopia as a tool is to use it to show what isn't there, to use it in a critical way. I have no intention for these utopias to be realized. They are meant to show what cannot be realized. I use them to try to develop a consciousness for myself as well as also for whoever might come into a discourse with me about them. It is about why these things aren't possible and then it opens up discussions on capitalism, urbanity and so on.
>
> (Dion 1998: 9)

Ever sceptical about the potentially disastrous realization of 'utopia', Norman limits his suggestions to mere proposals to avoid the dangers of moralism, the authoritarianism of imposed ethical positions, if not the certain appropriation of such ideas as still more consumerized eco-aesthetic lifestyles, where the utopian is channelled to fictionally solve socio-political problems (but in reality allows them to perpetuate). Such scepticism corresponds to the representational distance that separates the literalism of Norman's proposals from their ironic meanings. For it is the structure of allegorical doubling and referential duplicity that organizes his proposals. This factor explains the absence of any literal optimism in his work and reveals the complex basis of his utopian proposals, just as it structures his critical analyses of public space. In this sense, Norman's use of utopia, like that of irony, performs what Louis Marin calls an 'absolute transgression' that is uniquely available within 'utopic practice.' In fact, for Marin, irony and utopia share a similar structure of self-negation: 'Irony can be seen as the completely gratuitous loss of meaning; it annihilates meaning, every meaning, for its opposite. Utopic dialogue is the serious play by which discourse's signification is put into circulation to be immediately removed from it: its stable meaning is erased' (Marin 1984: 80). As a negative shadow of reality, utopic practice criticizes society and its laws. But this transgression doubles back on itself too, implying the reversal of its own representations. For Marin, the end of this cycle comes back to the real world: 'Its termination will mark the closure of the text, the end of the discourse and the beginning of revolutionary practice. Its abandonment is signaled by the return to real society and to the general ideology it produces' (Marin 1984: 81–2). It appears that this model is perhaps one of the few remaining possibilities for critical practice today.

In this regard, what Adorno once said about art's relation to utopia appears to be still valid:

> At the center of contemporary antinomies is that art must be and wants to be utopia, and the more utopia is blocked by the real functional order, the more this is true; yet at the same time art may not be utopian in order not to betray it by providing semblance and consolation.

> (Adorno 1997: 32)

Norman answers this quandary with his own 'cruel dialectic,' as a show of his was once titled at the American Fine Arts Gallery in New York in 1999; one between criticality and construction in which we realize that the more we experience oppression the more we long for utopian alternatives. It is not surprising that we are today witnessing a return to the utopian, yet a return not always as convincing as Norman's due to a frequent absence of self-critique or irony. For without it, we can see that what goes unacknowledged is the fact that such utopian alternatives often appear satisfied only through commodified solutions, so that the trappings of utopia turn out to be just as imprisoning as the oppressive conditions that gave rise to them. Yet, the refusal of the utopian may be just as problematic as its acceptance, as it results in an inadvertent complicity with the given socio-political and economic order of things, which is effectively identical to the potential naive escapism of the utopian, thus the cruelty of Norman's dialectic.

But can we propose any political alternatives without eliciting the utopian? Even those practices reduced to the purest negativity or based within the most rigorous denial of escapism leave a tacit 'it should be otherwise,' as Adorno (1962: 317) long ago recognized. Indeed, Norman's work shows that criticality might cloak its own idealism, one easily commodified as well. Unlike those constructions of utopia that function as the false ideological resolution of social and political contradictions (as in Hollywood film), Norman's work operates as the very agent in the comprehension of socio-political and economic contradictions, allowing us to understand 'why these things are not possible' so that perhaps one day 'it may be otherwise'. The doubleness in his project within and between critical expositions and utopian proposals, allows a number of positions to be pursued at once without a flat-footed literalism or realism's naïveté. As a result, a space is opened in which utopia and reality might suggestively interact.

References

Adorno, Theodor (1997), *Aesthetic Theory*, trans. Robert Hullot-Kentor, Minneapolis: University of Minnesota Press.

Adorno, Theodor (1962), 'Commitment', in Andrew Arato and Eike Gebhardt (eds), *The Essential Frankfurt School Reader*, New York: Continuum.

Alberro, Alex (2001), 'Blind Ambition', *Artforum,* January, pp. 105–114.

Baker, George (2001), 'The Space of the Stain', *Grey Room,* 5, Fall, pp. 5–37.

Bloch, Ernst (1986), *The Utopian Function of Art,* trans. Jack Zipes and Frank Mecklenburg, Cambridge: MIT Press,

Buchloh, Benjamin H.D. (1990), 'Conceptual Art 1962–1969: From the Aesthetics of Administration to the Critique of Institutions', *October* 55, winter, pp. 130–145.

Buck-Morss, Susan (2000), *Dreamworld and Catastrophe: The Passing of Mass Utopia in East and West,* Cambridge: MIT Press.

Burr, Tom (2000), *Low Slung,* Braunschweig and New York: Kunstverein Braunschweig/ Verlag Lukas and Sternberg.

Davis, Mike (1990), *City of Quartz,* New York: Vintage.

Demos, T.J. (2009), 'The Politics of Sustainability: Art and Ecology', in Francesco Manacorda and Ariella Yedgar (eds), *Radical Nature: Art and Architecture for a Changing Planet, 1969–2009,* London: Barbican Art Gallery, pp. 17–30.

Deutsche, Rosalyn (1996), *Evictions: Art and Spatial Politics,* Cambridge: MIT Press.

De Zegher, Catherine and Wigley, M. (eds) (2001), *The Activist Drawing: Retracing Situationist Architectures from Constant's New Babylon to Beyond*, New York: The Drawing Center.

Dion, Mark (1998), 'Mission Impossible', *Documents* 2/11 (Winter), p. 9.

Foster, Hal (2002), *Design and Crime*, New York: Verso.

Foucault, Michel (1979), *Discipline and Punish: The Birth of the Prison*, trans. Alan Sheridan, New York: Vintage.

Galassi, Peter (2001), 'Gursky's World,' *Andreas Gursky*, New York: The Museum of Modern Art.

Jameson, Fredric (1992), 'Reification and Utopia in Mass Culture', *Signatures of the Visible*, New York: Routledge.

Jameson, Fredric (2000)' *The Cultural Turn: Selected Writings on the Postmodern, 1993–1998*, New York: Verso.

Joselit, David (2003), 'An Allegory of Criticism', *October* 103 (Winter), pp. 3–14.

Levin, Tom et al. (eds) (2002), *CNTR [Space]: Rhetorics of Surveillance from Bentham to Big Brother*, Cambridge: MIT Press.

Marin, Louis (1984), *Utopics: Spatial Play*, trans. Robert A. Vollrath, N ew Jersey: Humanities Press.

Marling, Karal Ann (ed.) (1997), *Designing Disney's Theme Parks: The Architecture of Reassurance*, New York: Flammarion.

Mau, Bruce et al. (2000), *Life Style*, London: Phaidon Press.

Newman, Oscar (1972), *Defensible Space: Crime Prevention through Urban Design*, New York: Collier.

Norman, Nils (2001), *The Contemporary Picturesque*, London: Book Works.

Norman, Nils (2002), 'Response to "Artist Questionnaire', *October* 100 (Spring), pp. 6-98.

Owens, Craig (1994), *Beyond Recognition: Representation, Power and Culture*, Berkley: University of California Press, pp. 16–30.

Rosler, Martha (2001), 'Untitled', in De Zegher, Catherine and Mark Wigley (eds), *The Activist Drawing: Retracing Situationist Architectures from Constant's New Babylon to Beyond*, New York: The Drawing Center, pp. 15–26.

Rosler, Martha (2002), 'Travel Stories', *Grey Room* 8 (Summer), pp.108–137.

Ross, Kristin (2002), *May'68 and Its Afterlives*, Chicago: University of Chicago Press.

Sholette, Gregory (1997), 'Nature as an Icon of Urban Resistance: Artists, Gentrification and New York City's Lower East Side, 1979–1984', *Afterimage, 25, 2* (September/October), pp. 17-20.

Smith, Neil (2000), *The New Urban Frontier: Gentrification and the Revanchist City*, New York: Routledge.

Smithson, Robert (1973), 'Frederick Law Olmsted and the Dialectical Landscape', reprinted in Flam, Jack (ed.), *Robert Smithson: The Collected Writings*, Berkeley and Los Angeles: University of California Press.

Starr, S. Frederick (1978), *Melnikov: Solo Architect in a Mass Society*, Princeton: Princeton University Press.

Wigley, Mark (1998), *Constant's New Babylon: The Hyper-Architecture of Desire*, Rotterdam: 010 Publishers.

Notes

An earlier version of this essay appeared as 'The Cruel Dialectic: On the Work of Nils Norman,' *Grey Room* no. 13 (Fall 2003), pp. 33–50..

Chapter 9

Layla Curtis's *Traceurs*: To Trace, to Draw, to Go Fast

Richard Grayson

To watch Layla Curtis's *Parkour* is akin to watching figures moving across the landscape in ways entirely different from our own daily progress through towns and cities. On dedicated video sites on the internet, such as http://www.youtube. com/watch?v=jquXcwooV6A you can follow people as they execute breathtaking leaps and vaults, drop lightly down stairwells or jump massive distances between one high roof-top to another; to flow over walls, through fences and over buildings. The person moving across the landscape in this accelerated flow is known as a 'traceur', if a male or a 'traceuse' if a woman.

Each runner seems to deny the constraints of gravity and is able to move beyond the normal limitations of the human body with its tendency to rip and strain when subjected to intolerable pressure. It is like watching a computer-generated cinematic special effect such as Spiderman but with the breath-taking difference that no technology has been used: neither web generators in the palms nor wire flying. Parkour is an activity that seeks to make the miraculous actual, and which articulates deep fantasies of freeing the body from the bounds of the earth; of super heroes or of flight. Knowing that this is *not* a fiction, you laugh with disbelief, with pleasure, but your body feels its own boundaries, makes sympathetic gasps and winces as the *traceur* leaps to the ground some ten meters below, buckles and rolls on impact, then runs again.

Parkour is an activity that is exceptionally difficult to categorize. It has elements that recall skateboarding and biking, where a discourse between a human body and the environment is entered into and where each architectural incident such as a rise, a drop or a railing, opens up a different trajectory and its possibilities for response: whether to slide along, skid or leap. It is also gymnastic, with its somersaults and handstands and feats of strength, but unlike these sports, Parkour has no formal or overt element of competition; rather it is a discipline and an aspiration that seems to operate as much on an aesthetic basis as anything else: the aesthetic seems to shift between ideas of a stripped back purity and efficiency of locomotion deriving from the foundations laid down by David Belle who developed the discipline in France. More baroque ideas of flips and twists for the hell of it seem to be developing as it elides into the physical vernacular of the street-sport of 'free-running'.

The landscapes across which the *traceurs* trace their trajectories are often the bleak liminal spaces of modernist or industrial architecture. Places with concrete ramps, barriers, staircases that seem designed to direct and steer the human subject, en masse rather than as individuals, and which articulate human movement in terms of processing, delivery and outcome. They propose a relationship that is material, utilitarian and directive and are about architecturally policed access and the control of flow. Such determinations are ultimately the expressions of ownership and the operations of capital that have become more insistent as the ideas and ideals of the public sphere have been increasingly eroded and colonized by the forces of marketization. Such a framework of control is momentarily breached when the *traceur/traceuse* makes their mercurial path across an area. At this moment, it is transformed into an environment that offers possibility and pleasure, which can be subjugated and narrated by the free motion of an individual through the body; animal-like and transformed into a site of play.

Layla Curtis has documented sites around Westminster that are points in the vectors of *traceurs*. These are the walls and corners where they make contact that operate as landing points of traverses from which they spring off again. Rather than using a traditional camera registering the visible wavelengths of energy: colour and light, she has created imagery from a heat-sensitive camera that records the world in terms of temperature. Each screen frames a mysterious intersection of grey planes, an angle or a pale strip disappearing into the distance like a jetty or pontoon fading into fog. Each is muted, still. Suddenly, a bright white form flashes across the greys and blacks, in an animated body of light that briefly fixes on a surface to then immediately move on and disappear off-screen. This is a human body burning with energy. Where it has made impact and fingers feet or hands touched the grey architectural surface, body heat has been transferred from animate flesh to inanimate matter which shows as a white mark. The stain of light lingers, cools and fades. The rate at which it disappears varies depending on the nature of the surface – some materials hold heat longer than others – but also determined by how 'good' each runner is, the ideal in Parkour is to be extraordinarily light on your feet and this translates as only the most delicate smudge of white registering. Each is a signature: each runner leaves a different kind of mark as each movement has its own individuality. The time it takes each trace to disappear determines the length of each section of video in the work.

Layla Curtis has had a long fascination with how we understand and describe the word that surrounds us. She started out investigating structures and taxonomies of maps and making new landscapes through bringing together representations of regions that bear the same name or allowing names without outlines to narrate territories. Increasingly, in her work, the relationship between the map, the landscape and an individual journey has become a focus. *Polar Wandering* (2006) allows the viewer to see the entire journey the artist made to Antarctica by means of a line drawn on the globe, through information provided by Global Positioning Satellite technology in addition to specific incidents on this journey. You can zoom in at points on the line to see greater detail, on a greater scale and follow the artist's movement through a car park in the Falkland Islands. Some of these have images that you reveal by clicking on a dot so moving from the graphic description of a progress through space and time into the representation of a site at a specific moment and time (the accretion of which constitutes the journey).

Traceurs: to trace, to draw, to go fast tightens the focus further, to concentrate entirely on points of what otherwise remains an invisible journey. Sites where the line formed by an agent of energy – the traceur moving through space and time – has coincided with the inanimate world, to leap out of frame again back into the unseen. To see exchange recorded through the use of a technology that makes the invisible visible; that makes us aware of spectra and energies beyond our normal sensation serves to refract this moment through many different registers and indexes of understanding.

Each one of the actions that is recorded here, a leap, a landing, a traverse, has a name – 'cat leap', 'kong', 'slide monkey', 'cat balance', 'wall run', 'through vault' – and is part of a syntax of movement. Parkour is intensely practical, to do with efficient movement where discipline can free from the bonds of the everyday and allow one to transcend limitation by channelling energy into new and powerful directions.

We zoom in further… viewing the white explosions on the screens and the scattered fading trails of white, brings inexorably to mind the movement of sub-atomic events: of particles passing through a cloud chamber. Here, Curtis' images become part of the galactic buzz of motion and energy that constitute all that surrounds us, from concrete ramps to distant nebulae. That is, it is the register where we are made: out of the matter of dead stars. The fading marks in *Traceurs: to trace, to draw, to go fast* become the signature of an essential energy and the vectors of movement that they map are vital and fundamental in the operations of the world.

Layla Curtis, *Traceurs*.

Layla Curtis, *Traceurs*.

Layla Curtis, *Traceurs.*

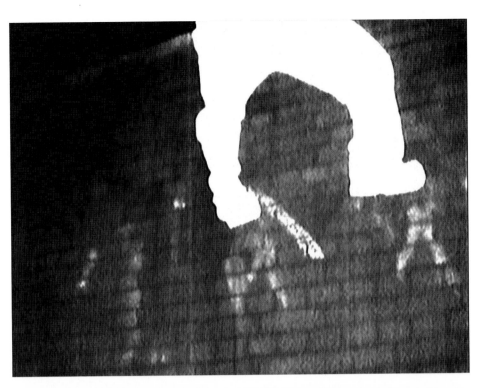

Layla Curtis, *Traceurs.*

Chapter 10

Oblique Angles: *Nonsuch* and *Nummianus*: A Conversation between Steffi Klenz, Jennifer Thatcher, Jeremy Till and Jean Wainright

Figure 1. *Untitled*, from the series, *Nonsuch*.

Jean Wainwright: Uninhabitable places, a dereliction of people and a disquieting sense of geographical location seem to be crucial concepts in your work. The places in your photographs are strange spaces to navigate and to find out where you are.

Steffi Klenz: Yes, my images do not frame a moment in that sense, an instance or people because I am much more interested to invest in the enduring qualities of place. So I always seem to depict a place as empty and not reliant on human presence. It is like Eugène Atget, who was commissioned to record the architecture of Paris in the nineteenth century, a time of exciting and bold changes in the industrialization of the city. Atget moved away from the ebbs and flows of the city to evoke a silent and deserted Paris.

Jeremy Till: I think this can be particularly said about the series, *Nonsuch*, which has a sense of absolute emptiness. You have to rush in to fill the void. Most architectural photography empties out the image of people on purpose in order to promote the image of the object, but what is really interesting about these photographs is that they take that attitude to an extreme, and so force one to look for the life that has been abolished. Because they are so empty, so abstracted and so evacuated of time, in a way time comes running back in again. That is what I really love about them; they take a convention of architectural photography, which is about excluding people, to such an extreme that it parodies it. And in parodying it, you need to re-populate it again because they are so uncomfortable.

Jean Wainwright: There is a similarity to the idea of the model village or the architectural plan that you appear to be playing with. We question whether it is a real place or not. We may or may not know it is Poundbury, but if we do know, what are we actually looking at here? I mean, there is that sense of displacement again and how we navigate that space. Where are we in that space, do we belong in it?

Jeremy Till: Most architectural photography does not allow you to do that because it is not as extreme as this. It is kind of the norm that you take pictures of buildings and they are empty. And that is it.

Jean Wainwright: But why is that?

Jeremy Till: That might be because in architectural photography you want a building to take the greatest role in it; you do not want to be distracted by people. Whereas in the photographs in *Nonsuch* the buildings are not the main subject; they take a secondary role to the relationship between all the different elements and the imagination of who might live there.

Figure 2. *Untitled,* from the series, *Nonsuch.*

Steffi Klenz: I agree with you. I always feel that architectural photographs are centralized images of focused gestalt but, I am much more interested in our urban fabric being engaged in the metaphysical questions of the self and the world. For me, the idea of the city must incorporate and infuse both physical and mental structures. So I am very interested in the values and beliefs that inform the built environment. *Nonsuch* does that, dealing with the tradition of utopia. The idea of utopia as the fictional imagination of the perfect place for the ideal civic society with Thomas More's novel, *Utopia* as a starting point is very much at the core of this series. But utopia is imaginary and I wanted to engage with something that claims to be the material realization of what often remains aspirational.

Nonsuch is located in the town of Poundbury, which is built on land owned by the Duchy of Cornwell and planned by the architect, Leon Krier. It draws its inspiration from English market towns. Prince Charles' ideas of the city, expressed in his catalogue, *A Vision of Britain* (1989), reviews modernist architecture as an inhuman habitat. So the town attempts to refer to organic growth, employing the co-existence of buildings from quite different periods and styles. The idea is that medieval cottages sit quite happily next to eighteenth-century classical buildings, mimicking the vernacular.

Jean Wainwright: Yes, the faux columns, the design of the buildings, the design of the place also plays a role in the way we are looking at it.

Jeremy Till: The Prince of Wales would hate that picture, because it has got imperfections. The tarmac is cracking up and all that is very honest. It is such a shocking image that it draws you in.

Steffi Klenz: It is also shocking because it presents one with a master plan of utopia that omits individuality and 'grand scale'. The place attempts a hyperbolized sense of perfection but for me it rather starts breaking. All of the images avoid showing you happy families or children playing on the streets. So I do not allow the images to bare any hint of idealization or collapse into sentimentality. I guess, what I am trying to say is that what has been planned and constructed in this manner, I see already as being in ruins. I always liked Smithson's term 'ruins in reverse' in this context, which is the opposite of a 'romantic ruin;' buildings that rise into ruin before they are built. Smithson must have referred to Walter Benjamin who recognized the monuments of the bourgeoisie in Paris' commodity economy as ruins even before they have crumbled.

Jennifer Thatcher: I love the two little bay trees in one of the images. It is again about aspiration: they have not quite grown up yet. I think that is become such a cliché in the last five years, having bay trees outside. It is tragic. I tried to work out what is different about all the photographs of *Nonsuch* and realized there are no security cameras, which is strange.

Steffi Klenz: Yes, but the idea is that the people who would aspire to that form of urban living and community would not need security cameras. You will never find any satellite dishes, burglar alarms or cables; so there exists nothing that could visually disturb you or destroy that utopian vision.

Jean Wainwright: You have previously cited other 'model-towns' and have been interested in the idea of what they represented and how they work with regard to the utopian city and community. We are really going back to a faux William Morris idea of what utopia can be or cannot be.

Steffi Klenz: Yes, Poundbury is part of a phenomenon in the history of British planning. It is amongst the most recent models of new towns like post-World War II developments such as Milton Keynes, planned and executed by the state. But it goes back much further. Projects of the Industrial Revolution such as New Lanark in Southern Scotland or Port Sunlight in north-west England are also examples of an intended materialized utopian vision even though those were planned and executed by capitalists for their employees. And what fascinated me was the idea of planning the ideal civic society and community from the drawing board, which seemed completely strange to me.

Jean Wainwright: I think there is an interesting point here about the artificiality of this place, which makes me consider placement or rather, displacement again. How do we know where we are? Well, we kind of know of Poundbury by now, so we should know where we are, but do we actually?

Steffi Klenz: The buildings in the photographs stand out in clarity, appearing in extreme sharp outline and detail, verging upon the unnerving but nevertheless they seem flat as if they only have facades. That always reminded me of Potemkin villages as if there is nothing behind those buildings' facades; as if they are painted simulacra of exterior surfaces. Some of the photographs might be of architectural models and I deliberately try to play with this edge of the space in-between artifice and reality. The term 'non(e) such' in English is only rarely used and refers to something that possesses an unusual singularity and I also like this in regards to the possibility of this place not existing at all. It is this careful balancing act between reality and fantasy that unsettles the viewer, not really knowing on what terms to take the images. Some of the places seem quite distinct in their over-determination but other photographs are quite ordinary, such as the photographs of alley-ways that look like they could be anywhere. The possibility of them being located elsewhere is important.

It is also interesting for me that in Thomas More's novel there is this encounter where Hythloday who found the island, Utopia mentions that: 'He that knows one of their towns, knows them all, they are so like one another...' I always like that when something intended to be characteristic and aspirational turns into something so indistinct.

Figure 3. *Untitled*, from the series, *Nummianus*.

Jeremy Till: Maybe we should look at *Nummianus* in this context, which could not really be located anywhere else but the north of England.

Jean Wainwright: Why is *Nummianus* so distinctive? What is it about these images that immediately say to us that it is a certain terrace in the north of England? What attracted you to photographing these streets?

Steffi Klenz: I wanted to make a body of work that continues with the idea of the abandoned city, from which life has mostly departed. Like in *Nonsuch*, I wanted to produce a photographic series that shows the urban fabric deserted, where things have disappeared and we ourselves within them. So I discovered entire estates of empty terraced houses that have been boarded-up in the north-west region of England. Most people have left these urban conditions but some people are unable to move and those inhabitants are forced to remain in the area. This exposes the last remaining inhabitants to extreme social exclusion.

Jeremy Till: It is hard to look at these streets and not think of the idea of a previous community. Whereas looking at *Nonsuch*, even though it looks like it should be a utopian community, there are no social spaces.

Jean Wainwright: Also closure: when you look at these streets and individual houses, you cannot penetrate the window because of the metal shields that have been put up by the council. There is something in these images that discusses the denial to enter this space.

Jennifer Thatcher: I just see these streets as absolutely full of the traces of time. It is a frozen moment but absolutely full of what has been there. The traces and signals of people, who once tried to make their life better.

Steffi Klenz: It is like the photographic plate itself: the surface of the city has received the imprint of events that has irreversibly transformed it. And this is what made me think of Pompeii in relation to this work. So for me these urban situations of *Nummianus* become an architectural and almost archaeological archive in themselves like Pompeii did. It becomes a palimpsest of present, past and future.

Jeremy Till: I think technically it is interesting that in *Nummianus* parts of houses appear twice. At first you think it is a terrace but then you think no, which just makes you look harder.

Jean Wainwright: Again you are being thrown off balance. Why the repetition?

Steffi Klenz: I was not interested in a kind of seamless sequence at all. There is this deliberate intention for the viewer to engage with every single house of the street. The repetition is never the same. Sometimes a window is repeated, sometimes I will repeat more; there is no exact formula, in that sense. The streets become fragmented and it creates a standstill in the fluid movement of viewing. So the houses overlap and one uncovers and exposes the crossings. The streets are then panoramically seamed to create a photographic space that captures the streets in their disjointed fragmentary forms.

Jeremy Till: Although you mentioned your work to be about the idea of the periphery before, it is also about extreme conditions.

Jean Wainwright: There is always that question mark – what is it about those streets and areas that made them vacated.

Steffi Klenz: The idea of commodity was very relevant to the work. The title *Nummianus* actually refers to an inscription found on the floor of the Siricio house in Pompeii. It shows in mosaic stones the names of the wealthiest companies that traded with Rome at the time – Siricio and Nummianus. Nummianus can be translated as 'coin' or 'money'. So I wanted to discuss these estates as a form of commodity because nowadays most houses in those areas are worth a fraction of their former market value. This is also the reason why some of the remaining inhabitants cannot actually leave their homes because it is not financially viable to them.

Jean Wainwright: You mentioned Pompeii already, the idea of the site, the traces left by communities; can you talk a little bit more about the relationship between those estates photographed and the excavated city?

Steffi Klenz: When I started working with these estates, they reminded me of a cenotaph, a memorial to the places people have lived in, the places also society has created for them. So the work very much became about 'indexing' of absent people and an absent

Figure 4. *Untitled* from the series, *Nummianus.*

community. Goethe described his visit to Pompeii as an impression of a mummified city and I very much see that also in *Nummianus* to a certain extent. The photographs highlight the red-coloured facades of the houses referring to the colour of Pompeii red. That was the colour painted on the walls of the excavated city, signalling a sign of wealth. I wanted *Nummianus* to comment on the former wealth, diversity and livelihood of these streets. These areas will be demolished in the future, so they will literally disappear, forgotten one day as did Pompeii's name and location.

Jean Wainwright: I was interested in Pompeii being destroyed by catastrophe and we talked about political implications of your work, so do you see a kind of catastrophic political event as having a destructive agenda on this work?

Jeremy Till: They are really tragic photos – socially tragic.

Jennifer Thatcher: The background is really interesting. We cannot help but fixate on those clouds, which refer back to an industrial past, a kind of ghostly reminder of some kind of industry.

Steffi Klenz: I really like this. As if the black volcanic dust of Vesuvius prompts thoughts of industrialization. Manchester, Sunderland, Liverpool they all have something ferric about them.

Jeremy Till: What I really like about it is your degree of obsession in the composition and technique of the shots, but that does not get in the way. I mean, they are very carefully considered images but that the technique is not foregrounded as it is in some photography. So what is emphasized in the work here is the content first and foremost.

Steffi Klenz: There is a particular image of *Nummianus* that is very important and carefully considered. No one lives in the street anymore. But then on the last boarded up window the tag name, 'Dean Connor' appears. I saw this as a meaningful and individual act of appropriation, like the last word of disagreement or rebellion against the public decision. His tag is like his signature; his last word and last personal expression perhaps. Being homeless means that you have no place in the world. But for me, Dean Connor still lives there in that house.

Jeremy Till: I am going to boldly now apply a meta-narrative to the work from a quote from a lecture I went to on 'All architecture is but waste in transit.' This is really interesting because it removes architecture from being a stable entity and places it firmly in a temporal context, always on the verge of decay. My meta-narrative is that the different series do that; showing a moment of transition from one thing to another.

Steffi Klenz: I agree with you. For me, the city has no fixed identity. It is subject to numerous demands, so it is always in the process of interpretation, interpenetrations and superimpositions, whose scale and rhythm are engaged in an ongoing movement of shifts.

Jennifer Thatcher: Are you asking us to consider historic facts or are you asking us to look back at a nostalgic time; to look back at mythologies? How in your view are cities built up? Are they built up of these factual layers or of mythologies? And are these mythologies interwoven – not just mythologies from ancient times but actually mythologies to do with our recent past?

Steffi Klenz: I am interested in the pluralism of perspective and ideas – a form of multiplicity. I always engage with urban situations in which individual and collective projections can become manifest. I do not perceive the city as just its architectural form, 'repressed' by its customary and socially regulated use. I am interested in the city as political and social signifier; an index of an experience and marker for lives lived. Italo Calvino's *Invisible Cities* conjures cities in the imagination and throughout his descriptions, he insists on the gap between the city as built and experienced, as it exists in the world and in the mind. That is what interests me.

Jennifer Thatcher: Do you see cities as doomed as so much waste?

Steffi Klenz: Probably, that is my attraction to them. Maybe I associate seeing the city with a loss.

Jean Wainwright: I think there are all kinds of different narratives in your work, different perspectives, different associations that everyone can engage with by looking at your photographs. For me, when I read these images, I find the net curtains in relation to the boarded up windows in *Nummianus* fascinating, because with no net curtains, people can look into your house.

Jeremy Till: Whereas I like completely different things, which force me to look. I like the fact that there are three little aerials on one of the houses in *Nummianus* and I think: three aerials, that is, a lot of aerials!

Jean Wainwright: It is quite interesting, the way one reads an image and the more you look at Steffi's images, the stranger they become.

Jeremy Till: There is something very strange in this particular image of *Nummianus*. Something I did not notice for a long time until I realized there is a motorway just behind the house.

Steffi Klenz: It is a noise protection wall.

Jennifer Thatcher: It seems more than a wall dissecting the house from the motorway. It looks like a social or political wall of separation.

Jean Wainwright: It is a division of society.

Jeremy Till: That is what I like. There is nothing accidental in Steffi's work: everything is considered.

Chapter 11

From the Melancholy Fragment to the Colour of Utopia: Excess and Representation in Modernist Architectural Photography

Nigel Green

Figure 1. *Fragment* series - Barandov Restaurant, Prague.

T his chapter will look at how aspects of the photographic process can articulate ideas relating to the representation of modernist architecture, configured by the anomalies inherent in chemical-based photographic processes and the practice of hand-colouring monochromatic photographs in the first half of the twentieth century.

My interest lies in how the ideological aspirations of the modernist architectural programme have been transformed by time and entropy into an object of history. I propose that photography functions as a privileged site through which to examine the 'afterlife' of modernist architecture and space, and by corollary, concepts of history, cultural memory and loss. I explore the meanings of 'melancholic' and 'utopian' to describe a dichotomy between the historic space of modernism as expressed in the ruin and its future ideological trajectory. These are framed as polarities which are also inextricably related within the photographic forms of representation of modernist architecture.

Process and fragmentation

As an artist, I exploited the fugitive potential and transformational qualities of the chemical changes that occur in the conventional black and white photographic process to develop an alternative documentation of modernist architecture. Emerging from the material nature of the chemical photographic process, I created a mode of operation which questioned paradigmatic conventions of the traditional monochromatic photograph. By fragmenting the different processes of image production in the darkroom and breaking up the sequential chemical procedures and timings, a play was instituted between composition and decomposition, realization and failure. The image emerged from this process in a dialectic progression of move and countermove that unfolded within different durations of light exposure and chemical development, its variability and inconsistency ensuring that each image is unique. The dual fragmentation of process and the composition of the images, along with their specific object quality, led me to think about the final images in relation to the fragment.

In *Architectures of Time*, Sanford Kwinter explores the nature of time and the changes it underwent in the twentieth century from absolute and mechanistic models to its re-conceptualization in accordance with thermodynamic and biological ones. Kwinter asks what would change in the arts and sciences if time was considered as a reality. In contrast to the rationalized, systematic and abstract notion of time designed to measure and master

Figure 2. *Fragment* series, Gloucester.

Figure 3. *Fragment* series, Versailles.

an otherwise 'senseless procession of events,' stands 'nature itself' as 'wild, indifferent and accidental' and which is better expressed as 'duration' (Kwinter 2001: 4).

The fluidity and transformations that emerge within and are co-existent with duration, can be seen as analogous to the practices I was implementing in the darkroom as a facilitator for the 'new'. The transformative operations that constitute these practices were primarily the agents of decomposition and de-spatialization that work against the systematic paradigm of photographic architectural representation and its replication of classical order. Kwinter argues that the diversity of modernist practice could be reduced to a threefold axis: 'that of classical time, that of space, and that of movement and complexity, or force' (Kwinter 2001: 38). 'Force', 'movement' and 'complexity' he argues, function to 'implode', destabilize and fragment the binary equilibrium of time and space within the system of representation itself (Kwinter 2001: 40). Time and space are configured in the photograph by the internal laws of the medium. These operate over a series of logical and sequential sites which calibrate exposure with chemical sensitivity. The corruption of this process is analogous to the notion of 'force', in that it functions to break the 'classical' schema of photographic reproduction through the 'complex' agency of 'chance and hazard' (Kwinter 2001: 40). These factors initiate an internal disfiguration of the chemical photograph, which opens it to an inclusion of another kind of actuality in the form of 'produced effects' (Kwinter 2001: 40). The represented object is transformed or dematerialized by the auto-destructive potential inherent in the material processes of analogue photography itself.

Fragmentation is an intrinsic condition of modernism and modernist practices from the perspective that Kwinter outlines, aligned with creativity and the generation of the 'new' (Kwinter 2001: 5). Fragmentation can be a positive force of transformation and evolution encoded within an innovative strategy of practice. The 'perpetual onslaught of differentiation' evolves things both material and abstract 'towards disuse, decrepitude and disappearance' (Kwinter 2001: 7–8) and the melancholic is also productive and creative.

History and photography

In Siegfried Kracauer's *History: The Last Things Before The Last* (1995) he asserts that history and photography share an affinity with each other in the way they represent the world. Kracauer suggests that history and photography provide a 'privileged epistemological space' which 'unceasingly erodes' the pretensions of philosophy to universal understanding 'by demonstrating its temporal aspect and its failure to comprehend the minutiae of everyday life' (Rodowick 2001: 142). The material reality that conditions both history and photography is dependent on subjective interpretation, giving form through transposition to the diversity of everyday life and making it accessible to conscious apprehension.

The subjective relationship between the historian and the photographer through modes of representing the world can be considered in relation to Husserl's concept of the *Lebenswelt*. The *Lebenswelt* determines reality as a shared communal and inter-subjective consciousness, which is constituted of all forms of human constructs. Intrinsically part of the *Lebenswelt*, history and photography make it 'intelligible through their structural correspondence or affinities' (Rodowick 2001: 150). Husserl developed his analysis from what he saw as the dominance of objectivist scientific thinking. The success of science had lead to the suppression of fundamental questions concerning its ontological and epistemological foundations with the result that questions such as: 'What is truth? What is knowledge? What is reality? What is a good and meaningful life' (Zahavi 2003: 126) were no longer central concerns. For Kracauer photography's ability to familiarize us with the ephemeral nature of the world is a demonstration of the *Lebenswelt*. The indeterminate and contingent status of both historical and photographic time is comparable with an 'anteroom area' (Kracauer 1995: 191) and has a provisional condition empathetic to the material documented.

The connection of photography to the *Lebenswelt* defines its unique articulation of the melancholic/utopian polarity. Although photography participated in the construction of the ideal and utopian image of modernism, its historical contingency reveals it to be

Figure 4. *Fragment* series, Kornhaus, Dessau.

a time-specific fiction subject to temporal displacement. The photograph establishes the utopian as a provisional proposition, subjected to the forces of history, entropy, melancholy and loss.

The modernist architectural image as historic artefact

The desire of modernism to eradicate the suffocating legacy of the past and replace it with ideas orientated towards the future was represented by Le Corbusier's text *Towards a New Architecture*. The symbolic order of the utopian is in the relationship between photography as a signifying practice and the 'ideological functioning' of modernist architecture. Reproductions and postcard images of modernist architecture from the 1920s to the early 1970s that have technical imperfections of printing processes arising from mis-registration in

Figure 5.

the four-colour separation printing process and colour tinting by hand evoke the provisional nature of the *Lebenswelt*. Some of the most dramatic and innovative examples of coloured monochromatic images, both photographic and mechanically printed, where produced to commemorate the many World Fairs and Expos of the inter-war period. Tait's Tower formed the centrepiece of the Scottish Empire Exhibition in Glasgow in 1938. Postcards of the night and daytime views were manufactured by Valentine and Sons Ltd. of Dundee and London, inscribed on the reverse, 'This is a real photograph.'

The original artwork would appear to have been cut out and laid onto the new sky as is suggested by the removal of certain details that were too delicate to retain, such as the flags in the right hand foreground and on top of the tower. The tree edge on the left-hand side also shows signs of having been doctored. The new nocturnal artwork would then have been re-photographed with a slightly tighter crop to produce the underlying black and white image.

Colour, excess and deformation in the photographic imaginary

New processes of colour registration through a single-film emulsion would render the process of hand-colouring photographs obsolete. Yet, for over a hundred years, the process of colour photography was subject to a process of perceptual interpretation: colour was conceived in the mind of the colourist. Julia Kristeva provides a psychoanalytical examination of colour in *Giotto's Joy*: 'In a painting, colour is pulled from the unconscious into a symbolic order' and 'irrupts into a culturally coded pictorial distribution.' 'Contrary to delineated *form* and *space*, as well as to *drawing* and *composition* subjected to the strict codes of representation and verisimilitude, colour enjoys considerable freedom' and 'excess meaning' (Kristeva 1993: 220–221).

Walter Benjamin situates the experience of colour in relation to memory and its childhood perception. In 'A Child's View of Colour' Benjamin suggests that childhood perception of colour is pure and elevated allowing for its integration into an 'interrelated totality of the world of the imagination' (Benjamin 2004a: 50–51). In 'Notes for a Study of the Beauty of Coloured Illustrations in Children's Books,' Benjamin adds that for the child, a picture book is a paradise and that 'they learn from bright colours, because the fantastic play of colour is the home of memory without yearning' (Benjamin 2004b: 264). The intense effect of colour is remembered over and above the objects or surfaces that were its source and it returns to memory as an aura or an infusion of a particular hue and saturation. Colour-like childhood is attributed with its own particular qualities. As a visual sensation colour serves as a medium for the imagination, memory and the notion of a paradise (utopian-other-space) to find form.

The processes that render colour, whether as a paint, dye or printing ink do not remain static and are subject to both technological development and the vagaries of time. In this respect, the colour of memory equates to the memory trace inscribed in the very chemistry of its physical composition such as that of a photograph or a printed reproduction in a book or magazine. Colour serves as an index of time; to recall colour as memory or to consider any form of man-made colour is to recall a specific moment in time and space. The chemical rendering of a photographic image constitutes a signature or hieroglyph of cultural memory. Colour postcards of modernist architecture are a conduit through which a time-specific concept of utopian architecture can be transmitted to the present.

Figure 6. *Fragment* series, Gloucester.

The photograph is a manifestation of processes rather than as a stable sign. By thinking of photography as a constantly mutating form mannered by external and internal factors such as technological development, economic necessity or artistic experiment, we can see, especially in the light of its digital transformation, that photography is constantly in the process of self-definition. On the surface, photographic images maintain a certain degree of constancy but at the level of their material and technological constitution they configure a complexity of factors that reveal the tenuous and continually speculative nature of photographic representation itself. The inherent chemical fugitiveness of photography articulates the provisionality of the *Lebenswelt*. In relation to a melancholy-utopian polarity, the photographic representation of modernist architecture is bound to the same conditions of duality in a play between aspiration and the corruption of material actuality.

References

Benjamin, Walter (2004a), 'A Child's View of Colour', in Jennings, Michael W. (ed.), *Selected Writings*, Vol. 1, Cambridge, Massachusetts: Harvard University Press, pp. 50–51.

Benjamin, Walter (2004b), 'Notes for a Study of the Beauty of Coloured Illustrations in Children's Books', in Jennings, Michael W. (ed.), *Selected Writings*, Vol. 1, Cambridge, Massachusetts: Harvard University Press, pp. 264–266.

Kracauer, Siegfried (1995), *History: The Last Things Before the Last*, Completed by Kristeller, Paul Oskar, Princeton: Markus Wiener Publishers.

Kracauer, Siegfried (1980), 'Photography', in Trachtenberg, Alan, (ed.), *Classic Essays on Photography*, New Haven: Leete's Island Books, pp. 245–268.

Kristeva, Julia (1993), 'Giotto's Joy', in *Desire in Language, a Semiotic Approach to Literature and Art*, Oxford: Blackwell, pp. 210–36.

Kwinter, Sanford (2001), *Architectures of Time: Toward a Theory of Event in Modernist Culture*, Cambridge, Massachusetts: MIT.

Rodowick, D.N. (2001), *Reading the Figural or Philosophy after the New Media*, Durham and London: Duke University Press.

Zahavi, Dan (2003), *Husserl's Phenomenology*, Stanford: Stanford University Press.

Part IV

Disrupted Concepts of 'Home'

Chapter 12

The Barbican: Living in an Airport without the Fear of Departure

Judith Rugg

Figure 1.

Reflecting on Marc Augé, Ian Sinclair's description of the Barbican in the City of London referred to the opposition between place and space created by its cathedral-like gloom, confusing signage and disorientating floor levels. Its bewildering expanse of architectural spaces could equally cause it to be likened to a cruise-ship, a prison, a department store or a hotel, although its long-term residents like to refer to it as 'the village in the heart of the city'. As in Venice whose residents struggle to make sense of space in a city locked into a prescribed frame and where 90 per cent of people are tourists, the City of London's 10,000 residents are outnumbered by its 380,000 non-residents. This chapter will explore some of the issues of living in the spatial paradox of the Barbican and its location within a global centre of corporate and financial power. Surrounded by the projected anxieties of the City to inhabit an unobtainable future expressed through a continual construction programme; set in a local authority which follows few rules of democracy, has its own police force and a unique electoral system, the Barbican as residential space embodies what Richard Sennett (1996) has described as the alterity of the city: at once a de-familiarization and a struggle for belonging. Where film sets abound and where 24-hour lighting ensures that time does not exist, a sense of 'home' in the Barbican is a concept enmeshed within an ongoing ontological and epistemological struggle.

In a brutal recognition of the fragility of human life against that of the endurance of buildings, the Barbican's statutory lease terminology dismisses any fantasy of immortality. It is *we* who are passing through (the Barbican was designed to last two hundred years) – we are not owners, but merely 'long leaseholders'. The home as an expression of the (futile) belief of permanence, stability and control is harshly dispelled by its landlord, the Corporation of London's cruelly direct legal language that is a reminder of the transience of human life and our place in the world. As fleeting as the daily city commuters which pass through its highwalks and plazas, we residents in reality are merely temporary occupants in a space which is always bigger, beyond and more powerful than ourselves.

The Barbican is an arts centre and residential space conceived as part of post-war urban planning to rebuild the City of London and the area around St Paul's Cathedral which was decimated by the Blitz between September 1940 and May 1941. Its late 1950s and early 1960s design was intended to create a 'coherent architectural narrative of texture, light and shadow,' which would 'emulate the grandeur of West End squares or the elegance of European Baroque, expressed in the Modernist style' (Heathcote 2004). The Barbican was envisioned to provide a new kind of living environment based on how its architects

Figure 2.

considered people should live, separate yet within the City and reflecting a 1960's 'lifestyle' cool of Scandinavian design, jazz, roof gardens and French new wave cinema (Heathcote 2004). Its 'revolutionary' design of podiums set above street level, three-metre thick diaphragm walls, communal waste-disposal system, specialized ventilation, underfloor heating technology and space-saving interiors were perceived within the context of the so-called progressive urbanism of the 1960s. Its 2018 flats include over 200 designs arranged around formal gardens, lakes and plazas and its three towers were the tallest in Europe for decades.

The period of construction of the Barbican complex between 1965 and 1984 was riven by conflict. It had been through seven planning designs and its completion was held up through industrial action driven by 'the lump' during an era when strikes in the construction industry rose to over 240 per year between 1960 and 1968 (Garlake

2010). Architecturally revered as a fine example of the 'New Brutalist' style, this kind of architecture has also been widely criticized for the disregard to the social and historical environments in which it has been placed. Brutalist architecture has become synonymous with a lack of social integration and failure to form communities. The aesthetics of hammered concrete, perceived as inhuman and cold, have also been seen as problematic in the context of a damp climate and against a backdrop of English leaden skies (Banham 1955). This and the Barbican's history of conflict between planners, construction workers and architects and its associations with social formlessness, seem to exacerbate its alienating effects.

The City of London is the area that describes the 'square mile' of the UK's financial centre, separate from Canary Warf and historically and traditionally the home of the major financial institutions (the headquarters of major banks currently at Canary Warf

Figure 3.

are rumoured to be ready to locate to the City in any current or future financial crisis). The City is made up of 25 wards governed by Aldermen in a system which was established in the twelfth century. The Lord Mayor (not the Mayor of London) presides over the Court of Aldermen and the Sheriffs to the City who are elected every mid-summer's day by its 108 livery companies (known as 'The Livery') which include the Worshipful Company of Haberdashers, the Wax Chandlers and the Company of Barber-Surgeons. Its non- residential vote (abolished everywhere else in 1967) gives it a unique system of governance. Dictated by Le Corbusier's functionalism and formalism, the re-development of the City prioritized the needs of city planners who developed an approach to disconnect future residents from the financial centre, resulting effectively in a form of forced social containment. From the 1940s, the Barbican, as part of this re-construction plan, was seen as a way to house professionals and separate them from the City's thousands of commuting office workers and traffic-choked streets. Its leitmotif is a fortress set apart yet still within the ancient boundary of the City walls and it manifests a kind of placelessness and separateness from the City which is already detached constitutionally, economically and socially.

The city, it has been argued (Leyshon and Thrift 1997) can be considered as a performing metaphor for the polis, where money determines the form and the order of life. The City of London is a hub for the financial (and ruling) body where the symbolic eradication of the individual is necessary for the benefit of economic power. The Barbican's position within the City has perhaps depleted its residents' sensitivity to social relations: a money environment, it has been proposed, dulls our sensitivities to place and social space (Allen 2000). The abstract nature of money and its architectural manifestation has the potential to further exacerbate our disoriented experience of space in relation to time. Simmel (1997) highlighted the problems of the individual in maintaining autonomy and individuality in an environment of overwhelming external (urban) forces. On the interactions between money and city life, he argued how money increases social distance and remoteness, creating a 'sphere of indifference' and a disassociation with social relations.

If the City of London is a permanently ongoing fantasy of desire for its corporate planners, the Barbican, with its highwalks and fountains modelled on Le Corbusier's modernist utopia of the 'radiant city', is a realization and manifestation of 'the death of the street' and with it, further forms of social distancing in its eradication of the unpredictability of human social relations. Disorientating and notoriously hard to navigate (some account the Barbican's low crime rate to its confusing maze of walkways and stairwells), its poor conditions for orientation exacerbate limited opportunities for social proximity, gathering and exchange and a sense of social obliviousness and indifference is echoed through the experience of alienation and spatial remoteness. Henri Lefebvre considered the city as a site to enable expression and free association: a space in which to reclaim the lived moment where the everyday is 'the starting point for the realisation of the possible' (Lefebvre [1947] 1991a: 27). Le Courbusier saw the city as a problem to be solved, rather than as a set of conditions in and through which dwellers could negotiate possibilities.

The Barbican embodies the modernist dream of twentieth century living to eradicate the disturbances of everyday life. Built during the1960s and 1970s, ironically or perhaps as a result of, during a period of radical politics and urban experiments with alternative living and reclamations of all kinds of spaces, especially the street where traffic was regularly brought to a standstill, the Barbican's overlapping residential and public space paradoxically largely eliminates possibilities for chance interaction. In Henri Lefebvre's terms, of-

Figure 4.

fice blocks and towers are authoritarian expressions of the commodification of the city by planners, architects and developers which create an abstract, formal and homogenous space that eradicates and denies difference. What Lefebvre proposed as 'a joy of excess' in the everyday as the site of the extraordinary and the source for revolution and social meaning, in the Barbican may be swept away every night and morning by the Corporation's roving street maintenance vehicle. On the rare occasions when Barbican residents do come together, it is in the formal context of the business of monitoring the ongoing encroaching redevelopment plans continually massing on its borders.

Michel Foucault conceptualized heterotopias as those places which reveal how society is organized and lived, as 'perfect, meticulous and as well-arranged as ours is messy, ill-constructed and jumbled' (Foucault 1986: 22). The heterotopia, he proposed is an enacted utopia that exposes and controls the disorder of everyday life and provides an illusory space in which to collapse, represent and contest all other spaces.

The Barbican's ordered and continually controlled and commodified space reveals and mirrors the abstract conceived space of the City that functions to limit the significance of individual or collective *lived* experience. As both container and contained, the Barbican demonstrates Foucault's fifth principle of heterotopias as that which have a system of opening and closing that both isolates them and makes them penetrable. 'In general, the heterotopic site is not freely accessible like a public place. To get in, one must have certain permission and make certain gestures' (Foucault 1986: 26) The Barbican's institutionalizing frame elicits codes of compliance and practices through which the epistemological becomes the ontological and vice-versa: framed, conditioned and determined by its specific spatial environment. Its support workers – estate staff, gardeners, cleaners, maintenance workers, car-park attendants and concierges – operate strict timetables and routines to control space to ensure the smooth running of operations to protect us residents against any inconveniences of material disfunction or uncertainty.

The Barbican is a stage – literally in its concert hall, theatre, art galleries and cinemas as well as for countless university graduation ceremonies, and the City of which it is a part is similarly an architectural 'stage' for economic power. Architecture is a way of framing desire to spectacularize the City and represent it as commodity: to produce a site of a single visual order that projects power and control over concepts of individual space. A continual process of urban architectural redevelopment and renewal creates both a fascination and an alienating dis-ease and dread for those in proximity to it. Within such a process of synchronous architectural immersion and isolation, lies the fear of the possible loss of points of orientation. The transparency of contemporary architectural panoramic space literally blurs all limits and boundaries which then become effectively erased, creating a sense of spatial dissolution and temporal stasis. Contemporary building materials, such as light-sensitive diodes that respond to the position of the sun and the changing natural light incorporated into the fascia of recent developments such as Ropemaker Place adjacent to the Barbican's northern edge, elicit a sense of simultaneous wonder and anxiety. The building's 84,000 square feet of trading floors; its vast, tiered

Figure 5.

landscaped roof terraces and commissioned atrium artwork of suspended strings of illuminated LEDs powered by its own ventilation system, form part of a new generation of twenty-first century, architectural aesthetic dominance. It is in such 'suffocating' panoramic perspectives, Walter Benjamin (1968) argued, that modernity is constructed at the expense of an individual, interior life.

The Barbican is subjugated to the transitory and transparent nature of the space of modernity which Benjamin saw as so invidious to human social relations. The alienating and decentred effects of such undifferentiated space are exacerbated by its proximity to the City's flows and movements that are determined by the repressive conditions of office work and commuting, subjecting it to the crowd's 'serpentine gait' during weekdays while being uncannily empty at night and at weekends. Barbican residents are exposed to the rhythms conditioned by the dual timetables of commuters and the programming of the Arts Centre, (over) populated at pre-determined times with people passing through en route to restaurants, the office or to the theatre whose opening and closing times regulate predetermined 'categories of absence' (Shields 1992: 187). Benjamin proposed the vagabond and the flâneur as figures who could expose such 'shallow propositions' of architectural planners by transgressions of different forms of boundaries and thresholds. Yet, the Barbican's plazas and highwalks enfold particular dominant confluences of space time established by office life or leisure, and inscribe a controlled space that eliminates any spatial conditions for social exchange. For Georg Simmel (1964), the contradictory experience of the stranger is one who spatially occupies both near and far and inhabits a remoteness and provokes a particular form of lack of interaction and sense of distance. In the Barbican, such daily periodic, overwhelming immersions and withdrawals of the crowd, simultaneously continually threatening impending absence and undermining any sense of permanence, make strolling not only unlikely but an almost subversive activity.

Figure 6.

In the City where banks, business and law and order reign, ideology and power are inscribed and manifested within its architectural representation. The abstract space of capital finds architectural expression in the representation of order through towers and office blocks. The fear of the threat of the unpredictabilities of *living* expressed though social or political contestation is suggested through the City's endless construction programme which continually pastes over allusions to history, instability and change. Its infrastructure and skyline, where its façade and 'mystical status' as a world financial centre must be constantly maintained, promoted and renewed, simultaneously traces a space of uncertainty within which the sound of pile drivers, earth movers and cranes resonate. According to Simmel, in the growth of objective culture, the individual is reduced to a negligible quantity whose sense of orientation is lost within the ambiguous nature of space.

Figure 7.

A continually changing horizon with the destruction and rebuilding of new developments has its invidious effects on orientation. The paradoxical nature of the City as a space of dominance, controlled and regulated by architecture, is subject simultaneously to the instabilities of re-development through which Barbican residents suffer programmes of boarded-up shops, transport closures and diversions, decommissioned office blocks and the noise of continual construction works. The most recent of these include the 23 story Heron Tower; the massive redevelopment site of Alphage House; the seven-year building programme for Crossrail and, at its eastern fringe, the impenetrable glass surfaces of 1, New Change, a vast 'retail destination' designed by Atelier Jean Nouvell inspired, according to the architects, by a stealth bomber and which stares out with detached insensibility.

Simmel (1997a) saw the most demanding problems of modern life as being the individual's continual struggle for autonomy and a sense of our own being and separateness from an overwhelming environment: the meaning of life within the city as an external and all-pervading architectural force. Surrounded on all sides by office developments, floodlit for 24 hours a day, the Barbican manifests Simmel's treatise of the dominance of the architectural visual. His proposition that in the authority of the conscious over the unconscious, the seen over the heard and experience over empathy, there occurs a disorientation from any possibility of collective life. In the Barbican, the distancing powers of such architectural space create an experience where the individual can literally be surrounded on all sides by closed doors. Even in its communal residential areas, any spatial incoherence is architecturally discouraged. 'Balconies' are in reality fire-escapes too narrow or too subjected to wind to sit on; hanging out washing is forbidden; pets are not allowed and musical instruments are discouraged. Occasionally, an illicit cat can be spotted or garden table and chairs appear placed outside, but the position of the colour-coded rails and regulation window boxes seem deliberately to be placed at eye level from a sitting position, stifling any sense of distance and obliterating any view of the lake or gardens. The Barbican's ordered space intervenes, rationalized by the rules dictated by architecture and 'heritage:' its listed status since 2001 further inhibiting, if not forbidding, intervention or alteration.

In Lefebvre's terms, in the field of abstract space and in urbanizing modern capitalism, time stands still. In the City of London, time is eliminated in its seamless interface with a global environment which is determined by international money markets. Like the City that envelops it, the Barbican's residents suffer the effects of a reconfigured space time. Time accumulates in a paralysis of history and memory, dictated by global markets and credit in what Simmel predicted as a 'thick present': a dulled continuity of the spatial in its annihilation of uncertainty (Allen and Pryke 1999: 63) and devoid of resonance. In the Barbican's urban hyperspace, all sense of the unpredictable is eroded in a permanently saturated, smoothed-out and illuminated 'now'. In such a false consciousness of temporal homogenization, sensations of space become hallucinatory, draining space of its quality and distinctiveness to produce new forms of separation and alienation. Lefebvre (1991a) emphasized the importance of the moment as the site of emotional clarity, potency and presence where experiences of revelation can occur. This 'moment' is non-durational, not to be measured in temporal terms, but through its potential for self-fulfilment. Everyday life, he argued should be considered as a potential 'network of anti-discipline' for chance acts and encounters where we might dis-alienate the everyday. In the Barbican's architectural modernist space, this dissolution of real time finds resolution, not in the Barbican as world-class theme park – in its institutionalized, programmed festivals manufactured with audience numbers in mind – but in moments of hidden *jouissance* created in its multiple performance spaces: through cinema, art, music or theatre, where a world of libidinal fulfilment in imaginary space is distanced from architecture, external to time and outside geography in spaces of non-representational revelation and intensity. What Lefebvre perceived as the production of 'generative moments' are contained beyond concepts of architectural space and its material measurements – truly, in potent spaces of propagation and *outside architecture.*

References

Allen, John (2000), 'On Georg Simmel: Proximity, Distance and Movement', in Crang, Mike and Thrift, N. (eds), *Thinking Space*, London: Routledge, pp. 54–70.

Allen, John and Pryke, M. (1999), 'Money Cultures after Georg Simmel: Mobility, Movement and Identity', *Environment and Planning D: Society and Space*, 17, pp. 51–68.

Banham, Reyne (1955), 'The New Brutalism', *Architecture Review*, 118: 708, pp. 355–358.

Benjamin, Walter (1968), *Illuminations*, New York: Harcourt.

Foucault, Michel (1986), 'Of Other Spaces', *Diacritics* (spring), pp. 22–27.

Frisby, David and Featherstone, M. (eds) (1997), *Simmel on Culture*, London: Sage.

Garlake, Margaret (2010), 'Prefabs and Stubby Skyscrapers: Rebuilding London 1945–60', in *Frank Auerbach London Building Sites*, exhibition catalogue, London: The Courtauld Gallery, pp. 37–55.

Heathcote, David (2004), *Barbican: Penthouse Over the City*, London: John Wiley and Sons.

Leyshon, Andrew and Thrift, N (1997), *Money/Space: Geographies of Monetary Transformation*, London: Routledge.

Lefebvre, Henri [1947] (1991a), *Critique of Everyday Life: Volume One*, London, Verso.

Lefebvre, Henri (1991b), *The Production of Space*, translated, Donaldson-Smith, N., Oxford: Basil Blackwell.

Sennett, Richard (1996), *Flesh and Stone: The Body and the City in Western Civilization*, New York: W.W. Norton and Co.

Shields, Rob (1992), 'A Truant Proximity: Presence and Absence in the Space of Modernity', *Environment and Planning D: Society and Space*, 10: 2, pp.181–198.

Simmel, Georg (1997a), 'The Metropolis and Mental Life', in Frisby, D. and Featherstone, M. (eds), pp. 174–186.

Simmel, Georg (1997b), 'On the Psychology of Money', in Frisby, D. and Featherstone, M. (eds), pp. 223–242.

Simmel, Georg (1992), 'The Philosophy of Money', in Frisby, D. (ed.), *Simmel and Since: Essays on Georg Simmel's Social Theory*, London: Routledge.

Simmel, Georg (1964), 'The Stranger', in Wolff, K.H. (ed.), *The Sociology of Georg Simmel*, New York: The Free Press.

Chapter 13

Defining Space – Making Space and Telling Stories:
Homes Made by Amateurs

Roni Brown

Introduction

The act of self-building involves the conceptualization, design and building of a home through undertaking all or some of the activities directly or indirectly through the management and sub-contraction of the work. Of the 23,000 or so self-build homes completed each year in the United Kingdom, the vast majority are created without architectural services. Although some projects are completed by households that have experience of the building profession and trades, the majority of self-builders, including those explored in this article, can be described as amateur. This chapter probes the experience of designing and making a home as an amateur, concluding that self-building is a complex and creative process leading to qualitative material outcomes (such as capital) and non-material ones (such as the development of self-identity and well-being).

The act of self-building involves the conceptualization, design and building of a home through the undertaking of all or some of the activities directly or indirectly through the management and sub-contraction of the work. Around 13 per cent of the annual new build stock in the United Kingdom is created through this way of building (AMA Research 2003: 6), and of these, around 94 per cent are built without architectural services (MacInnes 1994). For the majority, designing and building a home as a self-builder is an amateur activity.

The study on which this chapter is based began with a fascination for a practice that appears to go 'against the grain' of modern consumer culture which for those with economic mobility involves 'choosing' a home from the many options available. I was fascinated by the landscape of domestic architecture and at the prevalence of building that emerged as a result of personal agency, producing an array of distinctive 'one-off' designs that both engage with and defy the trends and 'taste cultures' of contemporary housing design (Ward and Hardy 1984). Studies that were pivotal in articulating alternative histories and practices of 'users' of the built environment, such as those by Victor Papanek (1971), Amos Rapoport (1968: 300–306), Turner and Fichter (1972), and Ward and Hardy (1984) emerged from post-Marxist critiques of the distancing of users from the design process which advocated the need for user participation design strategies. They argued for a new kind of partnership between professionals and 'users' such that designing might be conceived as providing a democratizing influence on housing provision. Interest in the history and practices of DIY-ers and amateur designers has provided new conceptualizations of consumers as pro-active creators of things. Paul

Atkinson in a special issue of the *Journal of Design History* dedicated to DIY suggests that making things has a democratizing influence on a number of levels, including the development of self-reliance, the broader dissemination of modernist design strategies in addition to opportunities for creativity and self-expression (Atkinson 2006). The literature on amateur designing makes clear the need to explore the value of everyday creativity and understand its significance within a contemporary social and cultural context.

Amateurs are concerned with outcomes but skills and knowledge are developed within designing and making processes where experiences are absorbed and expressions of the self are materialized. Self-building is a phenomenon where the discrete behaviours, motivations and roles of the producing-consumer are collapsed, bringing new opportunities and resources to individuals previously ascribed to professionals. I draw on six case studies of self-builders who made their homes between 1976 and 2001 in Hampshire, south-east England. What emerged from the case studies is an articulation of the value of designing and consuming differently in a user-centred way, producing often surprising, but commonly sustainable social and economic effects.

Conceptualizing self-building

The practice of building a home using the skills and resources of the owner and occupier is far from unusual in many places around the world, particularly where vernacular traditions survive. There are many studies that examine these processes in some detail, for example, Ward (1982) and Mathey (1992). The idea of self-building in Britain as a popular form of housing provision had declined parallel to the development of industrial and commercial building practices since the eighteenth century. However, despite this general shift towards a reliance on professional building activity, the existence of self-building continued in Britain and represents a volume of around 23,000 homes per annum (AMA Research 2003). The development of a recognizable self-build industry, providing access to information, builders merchants and financial packages targeted at the self-builder emerged during the 1980s as a consequence of the inflationary pressures that excluded the aspirations of many households from the mainstream property market.

The last two decades has seen the development of over 30 commercial self-build companies operating in the United Kingdom, many of them taking their lead from the timber frame building 'packages' developed for self-building, providing the self-builder with an array of 'kits' designed by professionals. In the same period, mass media fascination for 'reality' TV and DIY such as *Changing Rooms* and *Grand Designs* added to the perception that building your dream home is an accessible option. Although it is difficult to gain accurate information on the population and profile of self-builders, market research for the self-build industry suggests that the majority of those participating in self-building (some 66 per cent) come from social-economic indexes 'ABC1' (Chisnell 1991) and a contemporary market for self-building a pre-occupation of relatively affluent groups.

Information on the self-build market provides some useful themes in the consideration of the benefits of amateur building. First, this is a highly 'professionalized' industry, similar to other 'serious leisure' activities (Stebbins 1992) constituted by the acquisition of specialist knowledge and skills and access to a range of professional support services. Because of the complexity of building projects and the perceived risky nature of self-building, the industry established itself as the mediator of a number of technical, legal and regulatory elements. In this way, it provides a set of assurances concerning the quality and reliability of materials and the supply of housing models that meet planning requirements and 'professionalizes' the amateur's practice. Secondly, in defining the self-builder as 'any person, not known as a registered builder, who purchases land and by using his own expertise self-constructs, part constructs or self-manages the construction of his own house or participates in a self-build housing group to achieve the same aims' (MacFarlane 1986). For MacFarlane, self-builders are amateurs if they do not practice building as a profession or have professionally recognized qualifications. Although it might be perfectly permissible to include here studies of projects that have been self-managed where all or a great part of the design and building work has been contracted to professionals, such a study would tell us little about the knowledge, skills, creativity and self-identity that are developed through designing and building as an amateur. The selection of cases for this study was deliberate in finding those projects from which a rich account of the amateur could be found.

The genesis of participatory forms of architecture

Building developers of working and middle-class housing of the eighteenth and nineteenth centuries often relied on prototype or pattern book designs with an extensive range of styles, plans and detail for architects and craftsmen to work from. Nineteenth century eclecticism, inspired by earlier grand tours and from the rapid expansion of world trade, made building activity of all kinds exposed to any number of stylistic approaches. The building industry became more regulated and the various roles within the building professions: builder, craftsman, architect, becoming more discrete and new professions emerging such as quantity surveying. The distinction between various roles was highlighted by the number of professional bodies that emerged such as the Institute of British Architects (1834), the Institute of Civil Engineers (1818) and the London Master Builders' Association. As Powell (1980) has suggested the effect of this pattern of 'professionalization' which was later to include 'the designer,' was to make the contribution of individual craftsmen and trades more specialized. It also increased the standardization of houses towards 'universal building forms and away from local peculiarities and distinctive regional characteristics' (Powell 1980: 64) creating choice of housing style.

The intervention of the government, in exacting standards and limits on the building industry was significant in curtailing the surviving amateur building activity of the twentieth century. The Restriction of Ribbon Development Act (1935) and the London and Home Counties Act (1938) (Green Belt Scheme) resulted in much tighter control on the use and development of land on city outskirts and in rural areas. Later, the Town and Country Planning Act (1947) prevented further 'unplanned' development, which under this act included those developments that took place under common law and custom, including many contingency and plot-land developments. These marked the end of a tradition of self-help and self-building on marginal land. Such developments were perceived as socially and economically problematic owing to the high cost of supplying services to low density and low rateable property.

Inhabitants of housing schemes were rarely, if at all, consulted as part of the design process and many public schemes became a 'sign of the alienation of the built environment from the people who lived in them' (Miller 2001: 117). The momentum for change grew from a number of pressures that influenced professional attitudes to architecture. Cedric Price, Peter Cook and Reyner Banham experimented with popular iconography and debated the impact of consumerism on design form and theory, advocating the importance of participation in design. Colin Ward rejected the perceived authority of established professions in making decisions about housing design:

> We are groping both for a different aesthetic theory and for a different political theory. The missing cultural element is the aesthetic of a variable, manipulable, malleable environment: the aesthetic of loose parts. The missing political element is the politics of participation, of user control and of self-managing, self-regulating communities.
>
> (Ward 1996: 18)

Ward rejected the idea that housing design might be best approached by linking it to a particular 'aesthetic ideology', instead asserting the social importance of involving people in the design of their environments. Hughes (2000: 166) suggests that what characterized early opposition to modernist strategies was recognition of the 'basic issues of self-determination, self-build and participation that were deemed to signal the bankruptcy of modernism.' In addition, Turner and Fichter (1972), Hamdi (1991), Nobel (1973), Fathy (1973) and Papanek (1971) provided compelling cases of the social and community benefits of self-building, such as the acquisition of knowledge and skills that provide sustainable forms of housing provision; the value of finding local solutions to meet local circumstances by drawing on empirical knowledge; and the concomitant new role required of the architectural profession as a facilitator of others' design capabilities. John Turner reminds us of the importance of participatory approaches '…in the context of poverty, autonomy increases quantity: in any context, it increases meaning' (Turner 1972: 242).

Participatory approaches to housing design achieved some level of formal recognition by the late 1970s. A Community Architecture Group was formed inside the Royal Institute of British Architects (RIBA) in 1976 and in 1986 the first international conference on Community Architecture titled *Building Communities* took place in London. In addition, joint research by the Institute of Housing (IOH) and RIBA entitled *Tenant Participation in Housing Design: A Guide for Action* (1988) recommended that significant qualitative improvements in user satisfaction of housing could only be achieved when participation occurs at a fundamental level in relation to the design and planning of housing schemes. Much of this activity was orientated at making public housing desirable and durable, rather than exploiting the knowledge, skills and creativity of everyday households among all social groups and within the context of modern consumer culture.

Producing-consumers

Although it is widely acknowledged that theories of consumption have helped to interpret our relationship to the world of designed objects, particularly in relation to 'choice' what remains more vexed, is how, *within* modern systems of production and consumption, we find genuine opportunities to shape our environments in meaningful ways that are not reliant on *post hoc* processes of personalization. Research carried out as part of the Demos project, *The Good Life* (Jackson and Marks 1998) attempts to bring some analysis of what constitutes 'the good life' by comparing consumer spending against categories of fundamental human need. The authors suggest that consumer spending is targeted at those areas of human need associated with participation, identity and creativity (non-material) rather than those related to material need (subsistence and protection). Although consumer spending has continued to grow in the areas of material need, such as housing, beyond a certain level of provision, this tends to flatten out, compared with our non-material needs (associated with quality of life). The authors conclude that paradoxically, materialism inhibits rather than promotes the satisfaction of well-being

> … it is easy to project our own need to be creative on to objects that we can own, which other people have created – perhaps this is the inevitable conclusion of the 'division of labour', we can only glimpse the possibility of our needs being met through the labour of others.

> (Jackson and Marks 1998: 36)

The Demos discussion stresses the need to pursue development models that place a high value on qualitative measures of well-being including those activities that are absorbing, participative and creative, which satisfy aspects of non-material need and can support identity formation.

Contemporary anthropology, in particular the work of Daniel Miller (2001) has brought significant insight into consumer activities such as those concerned with arrangement, display and gifting, proposing that such activities offer the potential for individuals to re-contextualize objects as part of a personal identity. Whereas Miller's work has focused on the de-alienating potential of re-contextualizing activities, Colin Campbell's (2005) concept of the craft consumer takes as its focus the making of unique objects within everyday settings including those which are 'assembled' from mass-produced elements, as providing a form of authentic and productive consumption. Campbell, Miller and other anthropologists such as Clarke (2001) and Pink (2004) describe a consumer culture beyond and alongside the traditional ones of the consumer. This 'producing-consumer' paradigm provides an appropriate conceptual setting for an evaluation of self-building as a form of everyday (rather than professional) creativity.

Designing differently: Case studies of self-builders in the United Kingdom

Six projects were completed between 1976 and 2002, with interviews conducted over a six-month period during 2002. The case studies formed a geographical cluster in semi-rural and suburban locations in East Hampshire, around 50 miles south west of London, providing some consistent data about the micro-economic climate of the sub-region and identifying some common drivers for projects undertaken in this area. Each story revealed a complex set of themes: knowledge and skills development, ideas about self and representation, of making, crafting and toil, and the relationship with professional services, friends and family that constituted the distributed network of knowledge that brought a project into being.

The common starting point for each of the six projects combined a motivation to create more desirable accommodation with a confidence in existing skills and a readiness to learn new skills, confront risk and uncertainty. A key motivating factor for all was the aim to acquire a larger plot of land more suited to their needs than buying property from existing housing stock. A rural location or at least access to the countryside was a lifestyle requirement as much as plot size. An analysis of motivations to self-build implicated in the publicity material of commercial self-build companies clearly associates self-building with 'countryside living' and what is often perceived as a better standard of living than that afforded by urban locations.

A further motivation concerned the ability to establish a home on a grander scale, but with limited financial risk. Some were determined to use only existing collateral or to keep borrowing to an absolute minimum. They started their projects in middle-age and had very modest incomes. The need to reduce financial risk and retire without mortgage commitments appeared to be an over-riding concern for this group of informants. Achieving the desired space and location, at an affordable price, were key aspects that motivated the projects and stimulated some of the more creative interventions.

The acquisition of new information and skills and participation in often complex problem-solving activity provided a range of opportunities for informants to represent their risk-taking and creative selves. This involved desk-based work such as planning, quantity surveying and design and practical activities such as laying underfloor heating and fitting dry lining. Three were prepared to learn from scratch a range of building tasks and trades, and with some inventiveness. The more complex or creative these were, the more memorable and significant they became for informants in the narrative if each project. Stories were made vivid and memorable by the sheer physical toil and commitment of time needed to achieve these projects. The relating of stories about the building process makes transparent the elements of real work, discovery and invention invested, marked by the sense of achievement and surprise at successfully bringing complex and difficult tasks to conclusion.

It is in the nature of self-building, a process that can take substantially longer than the commercial equivalent, that many of the more detailed design decisions occur during the process of construction and even after occupation. Two referred to establishing the design in their 'head' and were assisted with the translation of their mental concepts through the services of a friend and by a drawing firm. The use of prototype designs (either borrowed or by reference to self-build brochures) and reference to historic patterns, also supported the generation of design concepts. The design process required a perceptual understanding of space and the way schematic information derived from sketches and plans translates into physical space. This applied to the design of interior space and the way the presence of the building changed the experiential qualities of the plot. When the existing dwelling was demolished the plot appeared to shrink dramatically because buildings generate a greater perception of space. Some found difficulty perceiving the height of rooms or how spaces would function. Difficulties perceiving space and volume was emphasized by 'on the spot' improvisations to a design.

In professional circumstances, designers use a variety of tools and techniques to assist the process of communicating a design to a client and to understand a range of structural, aesthetic and spatial problems. The participants in this study needed some basic tools to assist the creative process and develop their understanding of design problems. Referring to brochures, magazines and to existing designs is similar to the idea of a 'mood-board,' a design tool promoted by commercial self-build companies to assist clients with building-up a picture of their stylistic preferences. One created a cardboard model of the house and another used a CAD system to help them perceive their design as a three-dimensional form. Others used milk crates or hardboard laid out on the ground to get a sense of interior space as well as to establish how views of the garden might be framed by interior walls and openings.

To some extent, the amateur design process was based on empirical knowledge of things in context against which participants reacted – evolving and modifying the design through reflexivity. Great pride is taken in the way houses are designed and how ideas evolve. The design process for the amateur builder (and particularly those who do not use the services of self-build companies) is a highly creative (extensive, reflexive and improvisational) process.

Visual themes and representation of the self

The designing and making of a home cannot be conceptualized without recourse to ideas about home as a place of self-expression, reflecting our social attitudes and pre-occupations about the ideal home. The case studies reflected the complexity of making decisions about the visual treatment of self-build homes – the need to 'comply' with popular taste and 'in-keeping' with planning rules while incorporating the ideas about identity. In one project, the proximity of a Victorian lodge adjacent to the site was a prompt to base the design on a small 'Victorian' villa as a way to reflect a sense of permanence and 'age'. The local topography was mnemonic in recalling childhood outings and camping in the woodland to the rear of the property. Another refers to flints in the local area incorporated as decorative elements within the brickwork of the house. Another was keen to build-in a personal narrative into the design of her home. Reminiscing about a previous home she says 'we liked the Victorian house … we liked the feel, we liked the character ….' To reflect their identity with the older property one included a decorative bead of brickwork, copied from their Victorian home, immediately beneath the eaves of the house and garage. In this way, the new house could be located within a 'home history' drawing on the narrative device offered by the beading for connections to be made between past and present homes.

The adaptation of existing models and designs appear to be relatively common in amateur practice. Novelty, distinction, originality and above all, a 'total design concept' (or flow between all aspects of the design), are often present, but are not pre-requisites of amateur home-making and building. The desire to achieve an individualized and personalized project, however, appeared fundamental.

Conclusions

The amateur's experience is punctuated by a series of interactions with professionals who design the kits and the templates that self-builders adopt. They are the planning and regulatory authorities that define the standards of buildings and the acceptability of new housing designs, give advice or produce drawings for planning application purposes. At their most benign the duties of professionals within communities of self-build practice maintain the standards and professionalism of homes built buy amateurs – ensuring they are not amateurish. At other times, they are less benign, particularly in relation to planning permission, which can have the effect of reproducing conservative ideas about domestic architecture rather than providing scope for them to be challenged, re-invented or re-contextualized according to definitions of the self.

Media professionals are implicated in propagating the idea that building your own home explicitly supports the acquisition of lifestyle, largely by promoting the emulation of 'grand' or 'traditional' homes. The self-builders in my study provided evidence to the contrary – their approach is less one of emulation or conspicuous consumption, but one which references the self and everyday forms of creativity. Self-builders who design and make their homes are engaged in demanding and reflexive activities, the result of which is the making of a home that incorporates personal content and brings meaning. Self-building creates a home of greater utility and performance for the maker and through the knowledge gained from the process. Self-builders develop a range of knowledge and skills such as design, planning and building; deploy labour (their own and others) and can gain capital: between 15 and 50 per cent are plausible (Amor and Snell 2002). By taking on the producer role usually ascribed to professionals (whether builder, designer or architect), self-builders clearly gain from their experiences. In articulating the experience of amateur home-builders, a distinctive creative practice has been defined that brings rewards for households and an understanding of everyday creativity to the scholarship of design history.

References

AMA Research (2003), *The UK Self-Build Housing Market*, 2nd edn, Cheltenham: AMA Research, p. 6.

Armor, M. and Snell, D. (2002), *Building Your Own Home*, London: Ebury Press.

Atkinson, P. (ed.) (2006), 'Do It Yourself: Democracy and Design', *Journal of Design History*, 19: 1, pp. 1–10.

Campbell, C. (2005), 'The Craft Consumer: Culture, Craft and Consumption in a Postmodern Society', *Journal of Consumer Culture*, 5: 1, pp. 23–42.

Chisnall, P. (1991), *The Essence of Marketing Research*, London: Prentice Hall.

Clarke, A. (2001), 'The Aesthetics of Aspiration', in Miller, Daniel (ed.), *Home Possessions: Material Culture Behind Closed Doors*, Oxford: Berg.

Fathy, H. (1973), *Architecture for the Poor*, Chicago: University of Chicago Press.

Hughes, J. (2000), 'After Non-Plan: Retrenchment and Reassertion', in Hughes, J and Sadler, S (eds), *Non-Plan: Essays on Freedom, Participation and Change in Modern Architecture and Urbanism*, London: Architectural Press, pp. 166–183.

Hamdi, N. (1991), *Housing Without Houses: Participation, Flexibility, Enablement*, New York: Van Nostrand Reinhold.

Jackson, T. and Marks, N. (1998), 'Found Wanting?', in Christie, I. and Nash, L. (eds), *The Good Life*, London: Demos, pp. 31–40.

MacInnes, K. (1994), 'Here's One I Designed Earlier: How Architects can Capitalise on the Growing Self-Build Market', *Architectural Design*, 64 November/December, pp. xvi–xvii.

MacFarlane, R.D. (1986), *A Critical Investigation of Self Help Housing in Scotland*, Glasgow: Glasgow College of Technology.

Mathey, K. (ed.) (1992), *Beyond Self-Help Housing*, London: Mansell; and Germany: Profil Verag.

Miller, D. (ed.) (2001), *Home Possessions: Material Culture Behind Closed Doors*, Oxford: Berg.

Nobel, J. (1973), 'Contingency Housing', *The Architects Journal*, 24 October, pp. 976–1000.

Papenek, V. (1971), *Design for the Real World*, New York: Pantheon Books.

Pink, S. (2004), *Home Truths*, Oxford: Berg.

Powell, C. (1980), *An Economic History of the British Building Industry 1815–1979*, London: Architectural Press.

Rapoport, A. (1968), 'The Personal Element in Housing: An Argument for Open-Ended Design', *RIBA Journal* (July), pp. 300–306.

Stebbins, R.A. (1992), *Amateurs, Professionals and Serious Leisure*, Montreal: McGill-Queens University Press.

Turner, J. and Fichter, R. (eds) (1972), *Freedom to Build*, New York: MacMillan.

Ward, C. and Hardy, D. (1984), *Archadia for All: Legacy of a Makeshift Landscape*, London: Mansell.

Ward, C. (ed.) (1982), *Self-Help Housing – A Critique*, London: Mansell.

Notes

An earlier version of this chapter was previously published in *Journal of Design History*, Special Issue, 'Ghosts of the Profession: Amateur, Vernacular and Dilettante Practices and Modern Design', 21: 4, pp. 359–370.

Chapter 14

Remains

Lucy Harrison

L ucy Harrison's work is concerned with the subjective nature of our relationship to places and how understandings of place are bound to individual memory and experience. The artist reflects on how she is drawn to scenes of devastation such as demolition sites with their potential for metaphorical meaning about unfulfilled dreams or political ideals. She presents a series of despoiled places of leisure – abandoned cinemas, theatres and nightclubs – and proposes that like architecture, social relations are fragile and subject to the assault of forgetting, rupture and conflict, all of which can potentially to destroy the meanings of place.

Figure 1.

When living in Stoke Newington I often used to see an old Nigerian man who lived a few doors down from me. He would sit on his doorstep reading *The Mirror* and would say 'Good morning' to everyone who walked past. I began to talk to him more; he told me he had lived in the house for just over 30 years, meaning that he would have been my parents' neighbour when they lived in the next street in the early 1970s. He told me about the dance halls that used to be in the area, one in a nearby street and another larger one at Dalston Junction. He must have been talking about the Four Aces, which was later called the Labyrinth until it closed and was later demolished.

At Dalston Junction in the 1860s, there was an open space that had been cleared when the railway was built. It was used as an open air circus until the North London Colosseum and Amphitheatre was built, a grand building used for popular entertainment and performance arts, including Robert Fossett's Circus that performed with clowns, acrobats and jugglers, and Professor Collier with his giant and midget elephants.

Figure 2.

It had winter gardens, smoking rooms and extensive stables and the painted ceilings were described as 'bright, cheerful and picturesque'. The Roseberry Place entrances were decorated with carved heads of horses and elephants and 'being most conveniently situated next to Dalston Junction railway station … it turned away several hundreds last Saturday night' (opendalston.blogspot.com).

In 1898, the building was converted to a variety theatre and later it was turned into a cinema. However, many cinemas closed with the advent of television, and in the 1960s, it became the Four Aces club, famous for black music for 33 years, with musicians including Stevie Wonder, Desmond Decker, Jimmy Cliff, Bob Marley, Billy Ocean and Ben E. King performing there.

Figure 3.

'Long dismissed as a fading east London suburb with a chaotic daily market, a strip of cheap Turkish restaurants and a rudimentary relationship with street hygiene, Dalston E8 now finds itself the unlikely owner of Britain's coolest postcode. Its roll call of fashion habitués reads like a Who's Who of past and present design figureheads – Christopher Kane, Gareth Pugh and Marius Schwab have set up shop there, whereas old guard visionaries Pam Hogg, Terry De Havilland and Jimmy Choo are frequently out and about'

('Welcome to Dalston, now the coolest place in Britain', Paul Flynn, *Guardian*, 27 April 2009).

Figure 4.

In Berlin, the Palast der Republik has been demolished to make way for the construction of a replica of the Schloss, the eighteenth century royal palace that once stood in the same place, but demolished in 1950 by the GDR regime.

'... the building programme was for a house of the people ('Volkshaus') and home for East German parliament ('Volkskammer'). The project rapidly took shape. Architect Graffunder's team designed a large elongated box made up of a steel frame and clad in a reflective glass envelope, into which were placed on the north site the auditorium of the Volkskammer and, at the south end, a large flexible conference space seating 5000. The interiors that also included bars and restaurants were lavishly detailed, and the wide, double-height foyer featured hundreds of lamps (which led to the Palast's nickname of 'Erich's lamp shop'). The building was a success, not because it represented the state but because it offered amenities that were in very short supply; restaurants in East Germany were few and far between'

(Cordula Zeidler, *Building of the Month*,
July 2006, The Twentieth Century Society).

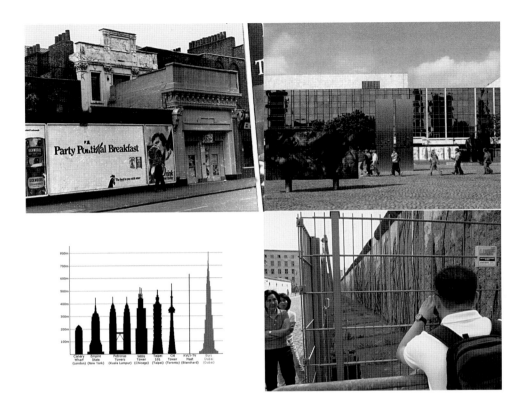

Figure 5.

The Palace combined parliamentary sessions with public auditoriums, art galleries, a theatre, restaurants and a bowling alley, but was only in use from 1976 to 1990, when it was closed because of fears over asbestos contamination.

'It was so beautiful inside,' said one woman. 'In spring, for instance, there was this huge carpet of flowers in the entry hall which made you feel you were in the middle of a dream. It really was a sight for sore eyes.'

(*Long Good-bye to Berlin's Palace of the Republic*,
Deutsche Welle, 07.01.2006).

Later, I found out that 35,000 tonnes of steel from the Palast der Republik are being shipped to the United Arab Emirates for the construction of the Burj Dubai, which will be the tallest building in the world.

Notes on Contributors

Roni Brown is Associate Dean of the Faculty of Design at London College of Communication. Her research interests are on user-led content in art and design and how amateur design contributes to well being. Her research into self-build, spatial and craft practice and more recently, brand experience explores concepts of the everyday in creative practice and design.

Susan Collins is one of the UK's leading artists working with digital media. Her works include: *Transporting Skies* (Site Gallery, Sheffield and Newlyn Gallery, Penzance, 2002); *Tate in Space* (commissioned for Tate Online and shortlisted for a Bafta Award, 2004); *Underglow* (commissioned for Light Up Queen Street, City of London, 2005); *Seascape* (De La Warr Pavilion, Bexhill-on-Sea, 2009) and *Love Brid* (a short film for Animate Projects 2009). She is currently the Director of the Slade School of Fine Art, University College London. http://www.susan-collins.net.

Mike Crang is Reader in Geography, Durham University. His research interests concern the relationships between social memory and identity, communication, space and place. He is co-editor of the *Sage Handbook of Qualitative Geography* (Sage 2010); *The Encyclopaedia of Urban Studies* (Sage 2009); *Cultures of Mass Tourism* (Ashgate 2009); *The International Encyclopaedia of Human Geography* (Elsevier 2009); *Tourism: Between Place and Performance* (Berghahn 2002); *Thinking Space* (Routledge 2000); and *Virtual Geographies* (Routledge 1999). He is a member of the editorial board of *Environment and Planning A*.

Tim Cresswell is Professor of Human Geography, Royal Holloway, University of London. His research is on geographical ways of thinking in the constitution of social and cultural life. His publications include: 'Place: encountering geography as philosophy' in *Journal of Geography*, 93: 3, 2008; 'The Prosthetic Citizen: new geographies of citizenship' in *Social Theory*, 20, 2009 and *On the Move: Mobility in the Modern Western World* (Routledge, 2006).

Layla Curtis is an artist whose work investigates the mapping of place. Her exhibitions and publications include: *Mapping New York* (Black Dog Publications 2007); *In Between the Lines: Recent British Drawing,* Trinity Contemporary (2006); *Mapping London* (Black Dog Publications 2006); *Polar Wandering,* Gimpel Fils (2006) and *NewcastleGateshead,* Locus +, 2005.

T.J. Demos is Reader in Contemporary Art, University College London. His research considers the conjunction between art, politics and global conflict. His publications include: *The Exiles of Marcel Duchamp* (MIT Press 2007); 'Life Full of Holes' *Grey Room,* 24, 2006; and 'Moving Images of Globalization' *Grey Room,* 37, 2009. He was the director of 'Zones of Conflict: Rethinking Contemporary Art during Global Confict': a series of research workshops in London and an exhibition in New York.

Tim Edensor teaches cultural geography at Manchester Metropolitan University. He is author of *Tourists at the Taj* (Routledge 1998), *National Identity, Popular Culture and Everyday Life* (Berg 2002) and *Industrial Ruins: Space, Aesthetics and Materiality* (Berg 2005). He is also editor of *Geographies of Rhythm* (Ashgate 2010) and co-editor of *A World of Cities: Urban Theory Beyond the West* (Routledge 2011). Tim has written widely on tourism, mobilities and urban materialities and is currently investigating landscapes of illumination.

Jane Grant is Associate Professor (Reader) in Digital Arts, University of Plymouth. Her recent filmworks, *Soft Moon* and *Leaving Earth* are influenced by astrophysical science and literature with specific reference to the work of Italo Calvino and Stanislaw Lem. Her other recent projects include drawings and soundworks regarding dark matter and a sonic artwork, *Ghost* – a development of *The Fragmented Orchestra*.

Richard Grayson is an artist, writer and curator. His exhibitions and projects include *The Objectivist Studio*, Alma Enterprises, London (2011); *The Magpie Index,* Baltic Centre for Contemporary Art, Newcastle (2010); *Cartographies*, The Performance Space, Sydney (2004); *Parallax Architecture,* Barcelona (2003) and *A Diary, a history, a walk up the hill,* Experimental Art Foundation, Adelaide. He is a founder member of the Basement Group and Projects UK. His recent essays on artists include Susan Hiller, Mark Wallinger and Mike Nelson.

Nigel Green is an artist photographer. His publications and exhibitions include: *Dungerness* (Photoworks 2004); *Calais Vu Par* (Museum of Fine Art, Calais 2001); and *Mind into Matter,* De La Warr Pavilion, 2009. He is currently completing a commission on reconstructed architecture in Picardy.